What Readers Say

"Garfield Vernon's work is **a scholarly masterpiece and a literary odyssey. He writes with a lyric and rhythm that commands attention** and demands that one listens assiduously to what he is offering. It is the personal journey of a man who 'aches for a better world,' his quest for answers, his dream of gathering the world's cultures together with the sole purpose of creating a life of harmony and peaceful coexistence.

"Imagine a world where peace becomes the primary goal of everyone's very existence - their *raison d'être*

"This, Dr. Vernon explains, can only happen, if we all increase our cultural intelligence and develop a fluid and intentional cultural competence.

"Throughout the book, **he mines the gold; he separates the wheat from the chaff and shows how we may acquire this intelligence and competence**.

"He uses an amalgam of his own experiences with diverse cultures, his eclectic choice of scholarship--formal and personal--his profound curiosity, and endless probing and analysis of theories and methodologies of the world's most renowned, social, cultural, psychological, and behavioral scientists.

"Dr. Vernon argues with Skinner, Freud, Marx, McLuhan and discovers Carl Rogers' humanistic psychology. He courageously challenges their positions, mines what he sees as valuable and discards what is not useful for achieving his lifelong goal of **reaching peace in a world mired in violence, discontent, distrust, and flux**.

"*Toward Cultural Intelligence: A Personal Journey In New Perspectives For Achieving Global Peace* offers you a look at cultural relationships through a new lens which considers the historical trauma of cultures.

"Dr. Vernon introduces **exciting new concepts such as cultural therapy, cultural shadows, cultural transcendence, and existential multiculturalism**. He offers a **thought provoking, tantalizing analyses** of cultures. My favorite is the analyses of America and Russia. His discussion of the Internet and its impact on culture is profound while disturbing.

"Dr. Vernon has given us a path and inspiration for creating a world of harmony and a reminder to ask ourselves, as he often does, 'What have I done?' "

-- Andrea Cisco, MS.

COO, Future Work Institute & International Multicultural Institute.

Co-Founder, Inclusion Allies Coalition

"Garfield Vernon takes **a deep look at cultural intelligence and cultural competence**, examining a comparative lens of multiculturalism through his own experience in several multiracial nations, Jamaica,

Suriname, Cuba, Guyana, Switzerland, and the United States of America. He examines the management of cultural difference, cultural shadows, and cultural tolerance, to explore what interactions, processes and structures can be put into place to foster harmony, when deliberate attention is given to building cultural competence.

"The book importantly recognizes that ignoring the role of strengthening cultural intelligence can weaken the foundations of peace and security at the borders of cultural boundaries.

"A cultural analysis is provided that makes a case for a framework for creating genuine relationships between cultures, through fostering common ground, engagement, and transforming attitudes as vital tools for fostering sustainable cultural literacy and peacebuilding.

"**The application of cultural competence capacity building identified in Toward Cultural Intelligence can contribute to a more transcendent and peaceful human coexistence.**"

-- *Karyn Trader-Leigh, Ed.D.*
President, KTA Global Partners

"Dr. Vernon's work is **a touching journey** of his own enlightenment in how culture is the cornerstone of peaceful relationships. We travel with him to Suriname, Cuba, Switzerland and finally the U.S. as he comes to grips with the hopes and at times challenges that culture presents us. Along the way we meet his teachers and mentors. It's **an intimate story that will have the reader thinking about their journeys for peace.**"

-- *David J. Smith, JD, MS.*
President, Forage Center for Peacebuilding and Humanitarian Education
Adjunct Faculty, Jimmy and Rosalynn Carter School for Peace and Conflict Studies, George Mason University.

"In *Toward Cultural Intelligence,* Dr. Garfield Vernon tells the story of his personal journey through several cultures and countries, shares with us the results of his scholarly research into whether training in cultural competence can improve organizational performance, and goes on to speculate meaningfully about the psychological and philosophical implications of our lived experience in today's multicultural world. While this sound like a daunting read, in fact *Toward Cultural Intelligence* is **an enjoyable, well-written, readable, thought-provoking narrative that should be on the bookshelf of every scholar and general reader interested in our cultural situation today.**

"Dr. Vernon's book struck both a personal and professional chord. Like Dr. Vernon, I too was born into one nation and culture (my beloved Ghana) and then went on to study, work and travel across the globe. I presently lead a supply chain consultancy firm and from which I criss-cross continents serving major international firms. My clients, my colleagues, my teams, every link in the chains of industrial supply that I analyze and explore are each rooted in unique, idiosyncratic cultures and worldviews, and it is my task to weld these distinct strands into a fluid, competent, efficient, functional whole. *E pluribus unum*: out of many, one. From all these diverse and seemingly incongruous strands, one weaves a mutually profitable ever-developing progression of interactions—a narrative, as it were, that supplies the world with food, medicine, equipment, services, all the things that make for a full decent human life.

"What I try to achieve on the level of business processes, Dr. Vernon strives to achieve on educational and diplomatic levels: he seeks to foster an effective cultural harmony among organizational actors that in my case fosters general abundance, and in his case fosters global peace. **Dr. Vernon's research has established what my personal experience echoes: that cultural competence can be taught, trained and applied to non-academic settings.**

"To help overcome the challenges of doing business across cultures, I established a training center, the Supply Chain Mastery Academy, where students from all over the world are trained by teachers from differing cultures not only in the technical competences of the profession, but also in the nuances and fluencies of international multicultural human interaction.

"What Dr. Vernon has established thrugh his scholarship, I witness every day in professional practice: cultural competence can be taught, people from different backgrounds can learn to work together in enjoyable productive harmony.

"Like Dr. Vernon, I too have found that such lessons

are best communicated in narrative forms. We learn better from stories and people than from abstractions. In my novels, *Chaotic Butterfly* and *Devil In The Chain*, I trace the conflicts and cooperations of individuals of various backgrounds as they strive to achieve their larger goals. My cast is multinational and multicultural, the settings global, but they are tales of the concrete, my reflections concentrated in characters and actions. In *Toward Cultural Intelligence*, Dr. Vernon's journey takes a complimentary path, rising from direct experience and memoir to take a more theoretical wing.

"But that is not a contradiction. Thought and action work best in unison. Whether applied to corporate, academic or social institutions, *Toward Cultural Intelligence* is **a guidebook for those seeking to forge that unity, and to bring reason and lived experience together in one vivid whole.**

"Cultural intelligence, in broad terms, may well be the key to our survival as a species. Dr. Vernon is to be commended for enhancing our grasp of its nature and possibilities, and taking our understanding further."

— *James Amoah*
B.Sc. Pharmacology; M.Sc. Operational Research
President, Supply Chain Mastery Academy
CEO, Kaleidoscope SARL

"Garfield Vernon's new book, *Toward Cultural Intelligence: A Personal Journey In New Perspectives*

For Achieving Global Peace, is **a brilliant, articulate, compassionate guide on how to achieve and maintain one's cultural competenc**e on a planet transformed by technology. Dr. Vernon is a mentor and a guide with scope and compassion. **Like his countryman Bob Marley, he combats despair with spiritual illumination and existential spark.**"

    -- Peter Lownds, Ph.D.
      Co-Founder, The Paulo Freire Institute, UCLA

TOWARD CULTURAL INTELLIGENCE

TOWARD CULTURAL INTELLIGENCE

A
Personal Journey
In
New Perspectives
For
Achieving
Global Peace

Pascal Editions 2022

Towards Cultural Intelligence:
A Personal Jourey In New Perspectives
For Achieving Global Peace

A Pascal Editions Book / May 2022

Copyright @ 2022 by Garfield Vernon

First Edition Published by
Pascal Editions
Rochester New York

Layout and Cover Design by Pascal Editions

Dedication

I dedicate this book to my son, Seth, a sophomore in high school. Of all the special gifts of life, however great or small, to have you as my son, is the greatest gift of all. You are kind, loving, funny and true. I am grateful beyond words for the happiness which you have brought me and your mother. I love you deeply, Son, and I thank you for adding so much joy and laughter to my life!

I also dedicate this book to my parents. To my father Sylvester, in his memoriam, who instilled in me from an early age to love and respect all humankind. To my mother Jean (Pat), whose lifetime of sacrifice and undying support have been tremendous. I owe a debt of gratitude and appreciation to you for selflessly giving me so much of yourself. All my love, mother!

"...great principles, great ideals
know no nationality."

- Marcus Garvey

Acknowledgements

An abundance of thanks to my family for your eternal support. You have been my rock throughout this writing process. You have been there for me when I needed you most. Love always!

Thanks to my close friends. Fellows, in addition to our camaraderie, you each are intellectually bold and never ones to shy away from topics that might prove controversial or non-conforming. This book in part is made possible because of your support.

A special thanks to these three gentlemen—Dr. Gordon Cowans (Jamaica), Dr. Osbourne Murray (Toronto), and Dr. Okechuku Ugwu (Atlanta)—for not only the countless and thoughtful discussions I've had with each of you, but also for your inherent abilities to listen and to offer points of views based on measured wisdom.

Thanks to all my readers who over the years have taken the time and made the effort to not just read my postings, but send detailed comments and feedback.

Thanks to The United Church in Jamaica and the Cayman Islands (UCJCI). As a body, you understood both the reality of a rapidly changing world and the complex history of religious activity. Thank you for having provided me several opportunities to engage with culturally different others.

Thanks to the United Nations, and in particular, Lily, my Supervisor at UNESCO. My time there was evolutionary, to say the least! Working there I gained new perspectives on a range of issues including a culture of peace, advocacy in conflict-affected areas, education and culture, education for sustainable development, global citizenship, global literacy, human rights and international solidarity, peace-building, and the rights of persons who are of national or ethnic origin, religious and linguistic minorities.

To the United States Institute of Peace (USIP) for giving me information and access—via your online self-paced courses—to resources and tools available for peace-builders. Thank you.

The University of Maryland Center for International Development & Conflict Management (CIDCM). I am happy to have attended and followed a number of your sessions, research, and policy publications that are pertinent to addressing critical global concerns. Thank you.

Thanks to Professors Stephen Klees and Jing Lin in the International Education Policy Program (within the Department of Counseling, Higher Education, and Special Education - CHSE) at the University of Maryland for inviting me to participate in your ProSeminars dealing with the challenges and possibilities of education within a global culture.

Dean Alpaslan Ozerdem, and the Jimmy and Rosalynn Carter School for Peace and Conflict Resolution at George Mason University. For years I've been reading your national and international impact studies examining the causes and nature of conflict throughout the world. Thank you.

Thanks to Dr. Tapio Kanninen and the Global Crisis Information Network (GCINET). Your seminars, presentations, and the conversations I've had with you have proven invaluable to my own quest to find innovative solutions to our interrelated global threats.

Reverend Karen Dickman and the Institute for Multi-Track Diplomacy (IMTD). I appreciate the period of time I worked there, though brief. Thanks too for your unique approach to peace-building which aims at uncovering the deprivation of basic human needs, thus involving many interconnected individuals, activities, and parts.

Ms. Elizabeth Hume, and the Alliance for Peacebuilding (AfP). Thanks for making available to the public your annual reports that address your work, accomplishments, and vision for the future.

Mr. Steve Killelea and the Institute for Economics & Peace (IEP). Thanks for your vision of humanity, understanding of positive peace, and for developing the global and national indices of peace, which provided me with rich data regarding the economic cost of violence.

Dr. Hyun Jin Preston Moon and the Global Peace Foundation (GPF) whose work in chapters around the world—to realize interfaith understanding, strengthen family values, and promote a culture of service—I've been following. Thank you.

Mr. James Patton and the International Center on Religion and Diplomacy (ICRD). Thanks for your work that supports part of the book's strategy regarding theologies, polities, histories, and spiritual cultures having a critical role to play in how social realities and structures of society are transformed for peace and peacemaking.

Ms. Diane Tate and The Peace Alliance. I learned a lot from your comprehensive and collaborative approach to peace and peace-building. Thank you.

Mr. Paul Turner and the Fund for Peace (FFP). Your years of work in sustainable security gave me helpful insights into the importance of contextual risk assessment necessary for global peace.

TABLE OF CONTENTS

Foreword

Becoming
We
The
Peoples

by

Patricia M. Miche, Ed.D.

FOREWORD

Becoming We The Peoples:

Journey into a Multicultural World Community

By Patricia M. Mische, Ed.D.

Journeys can begin with a few steps – or a few words --and end in your soul. They can be walked alone or alongside millions. They can meet obstacles that require one to overcome and continue with greater strength. They can transform individuals. They can transform the world.

This book is an account of one person's journey of discovery in a fast-changing, multicultural world. Millions of others have, are, and will make similar journeys. For, in a world where almost 8 billion people share one planetary home and depend on one another for their ecological, economic, social, physical, mental, and spiritual well-being, it is no longer possible to be isolated from other cultures. Nor is it in one's self-interest to try. Our mutual security and well-being now require forging pathways in multi-cultural understanding, cooperation, and peace building. The journey before us is not one of abandoning our diverse cultural identities, but of bridging divisions, finding common ground, advancing mutual enrichment, and developing a more profound sense of self and our humanity through engagement with the other.

Journeys like this have been taken before, but never on such a global scale. More than two centuries ago disparate and disunited peoples in thirteen American colonies faced similar challenges as they struggled for self-determination and democratic freedoms. And for the past eight decades a global collective journey fostering multicultural approaches to greater peace and security has been underway on pathways opened through the United Nations.

"We the People." Thus begins the Constitution of the United States of America. With these three words diverse people in this new country took the first steps in a still ongoing journey toward a more perfect union. The words were a vision of a not yet, but possible, future. "We the people." The words hung over the horizon like a magnet attracting people toward the realization of greater human dignity and fulfillment.

At the beginning of the journey into a United States, the "We" in "We the People" was not inclusive. The people were fractured along a thousand fault lines. People in separate colonies came from separate backgrounds, beliefs, classes, and cultural identities. There were Puritan, Anglican, Catholic, Indigenous, European, African, Asian, Hispanic, and Creole identities. There were slave owners and slaves; aristocrats and indentured servants; faiths and races that "belonged," and those that were not tolerated. Male property holders could vote but not male slaves or servants, not indigenous people, and not women of any race or class. "We the people" was not yet a reality, but a destination. Some undertook the journey in hope and joy. Others, fearful of sharing power and privilege, resisted and obstructed pathways to a more inclusive "we the people." The price of not joining the journey toward a more perfect union would be recurring discontent, conflict, frustrated dreams, unrealized potential, fractured communities, and stunted human beings.

The United Nations, like the United States, was launched on its journey with the starting words "We the Peoples." The added "s" underscores the multiplicity of the world's peoples and their cultures, then and now.

WWII had been the most horrific war in human history. Millions had been killed. Homes, cities, and cultural artifacts turned to rubble. Economic and social conditions were desperate. The world's peoples were hungry for bread and an end to war. Thus, the opening words of the Preamble, "We the Peoples of the United Nations, determined to save succeeding generations from the scourge of war...," were a fitting way for peoples sick of war to start on a journey toward a world without war.

But, as in the U.S. Constitution, these words heading the UN Charter were more prophetic vision than starting reality. Indeed, the words came late in the drafting process. Initial drafts of the Preamble began "The High Contracting Parties . . .." This was because the United Nations was to be a state-centric organization – i.e., an organization of, by and for nation states. Its Charter upholds national sovereignty as one of its core principles. The UN is not a government. It cannot tell member states what to do. The member states tell the UN what to do. The UN has almost no enforcement power. It relies on the good will of its member states to abide by the norms, rules, and procedures they have agreed to in the Charter and subsequent international agreements.

However, while the UN Charter is essentially state-centric, its Preamble, beginning with the words "We the peoples," is human-centric. It underscores the dignity of human beings of all nations, classes, races, genders, and cultures, regardless of their citizenship or the states which govern them. It underscores the sovereignty and rights of individual human beings.

Work on conceptualizing and drafting the UN Charter began even before the end of the most horrific war in human history, a war that its predecessor, the League of Nations was too weak to prevent. The UN Charter seeks to correct some of the League's weaknesses, going as far as states-parties would agree to go at the time in developing stronger norms and structures for safeguarding world peace and security.

The vision of peace and security articulated in the Preamble to the UN Charter is more comprehensive than that of its failed predecessor. Whereas the League focused primarily on collective security through arms control and war prevention (peace as the absence of war, or "negative" peace), the Preamble and Article 1 (Purposes) of the UN Charter includes but adds to this a vision of positive peace – i.e. the presence of positive conditions for upholding human dignity and preventing war, including social and economic well-being, self-determination, and "human rights and fundamental freedoms for all without distinction as to race, sex, language or religion." It also aims to achieve "international cooperation in solving international problems of an economic, social, cultural and humanitarian character" and to promote tolerance and learning to live together as good neighbors."

The United Nations is still on its journey. What was established in 1945 was not to be its final form or agenda. Since its founding the number of member states has grown from 51 to 193, encompassing almost all the world's countries, cultures and 8 billion people. Moreover, the UN has been a major vehicle for international agreements and cooperation in addressing critical human issues, from arms control, decolonization, world trade and finance, economic development, food, health, and refugees, to the improved status of women and children, and human rights, to name only a few.

These issue areas were foreseen in the aims articulated in the UN Charter. Parallel to the UN and in relationship with it, Specialized Agencies, Programs and Funds were established to address these issue areas (e.g., the United Nations Educational, Scientific and Cultural Organization (UNESCO), the World Health Organization, the World Food and Agricultural Program, the World Bank, the International Monetary Fund, UNICEF, the UN Development Program, the Office of the High Commissioner for Human Rights, to name a few). Over the almost 8 decades since the Charter was adopted and the UN and its related agencies and programs began their interactive work, significant progress has been made in these areas. The UN has gathered scientific information, convened international conferences, succeeded in getting member states to agree to goals, standards, international laws, educational and action programs, funding, and collaborative work in all these areas. Although there have been shortfalls in member states living up to all their agreements, thanks to the UN, over the last eight decades there has been an unprecedented level of global cooperation in work for our common future.

Although the UN has been constrained in some areas (e.g., by the veto power of the permanent members of the Security Council), it has been like a living organism in other areas, able to adjust and respond to new issues not foreseen when its Charter was drafted, and also living up to the words "We the Peoples" by accommodating, even inviting, an ever increasing role for civil society and nongovernmental organizations.

Environmental protection, a prohibition on land mines, and the Culture of Peace Programme are a few of many examples of originally unforeseen issues that were brought into the UN through the words "We the Peoples."

In 1945, few foresaw the need for the UN Charter to include environmental protection as a critical aspect of global peace and security. But as ecological threats became more manifest in the 1960s, people began organizing from the ground up in countries all over the world, calling their local and national governments to enact environmental protection policies, and also pressing the UN to enact global level policies.

Ecological threats cannot be contained within national borders. Nor can national policies alone effectively redress them. Global level policies are needed.

In response, the UN convened world conferences and brokered international agreements, including agreements to protect the ozone layer, biodiversity, forests, and trans-boundary waters; to govern the trans-boundary shipment of toxic wastes, to address climate change, to advance environmentally sustainable development, and more. It also established the United Nations Environmental Programme (UNEP) and encouraged member states to establish environmental protection programs in their respective countries. It is an example of how "we the peoples" can and have led the way in meeting global challenges and advancing global policy development.

Citizen groups also led the way for a ban on land mines. Used widely in WWII and later wars, land mines were killing and maiming people long after the wars ended. Led by six nongovernmental organizations who established the International Campaign to Ban Land Mines (ICBL) in 1991, ordinary people networked and collaborated cross culturally around the world to raise public awareness and support, and to move their agenda to the UN, leading to the drafting and adoption of the Convention on the Prohibition of the Use, Stockpiling, Production and Transfer of Anti-Personnel Mines and on their Destruction. To date, 164 countries have signed and become parties to the convention. The Campaign, with thousands of members working collaboratively cross nationally, monitors compliance and continues to press the 33 countries who have not yet ratified the treaty (including China, Russia, and the United States) to do so.

The UN Culture of Peace Programme is another

example. Beginning in the 1980s, the vision for this program rose from nongovernmental groups to UNESCO where it was adopted in 1992, and thence to the UN General Assembly which, in 1999, unanimously adopted the Declaration and Programme of Action on a Culture of Peace (A/RES/53/243). This was followed by the International Year for the Culture of Peace in the Year 2000, and the International Decade for a Culture of Peace and Non-Violence for the Children of the World (2001-2010). The UN defines a culture of peace as "a set of values, attitudes, traditions and modes of behaviors and ways of life that reject violence and prevent conflicts by tackling their root causes to solve problems through dialogue and negotiation among individuals, groups and nations." (UN Resolution A/RES/52/13).

The action program for a Culture of Peace includes: education; environmentally sustainable economic and social development; respect for human rights; equality of women and men; democratic participation; intercultural understanding, tolerance and solidarity; the free flow of information and knowledge; and international peace and security. These action areas have been priorities of the UN since its founding, but in the Culture of Peace program they are linked into one coherent concept of nonviolence and peace.

This program opened new levels of cooperation between civil society and UN agencies. It has broadened the meaning of, and participation in, global governance. The program came from below, from the hearts and minds of "we the people." And it has engaged millions of people from diverse cultures in villages and cities, businesses, professional associations, schools, and religious communities around the world in cross cultural collaboration with UN agencies in the work of peace building. It has truly been a program of, by, and for "we the peoples."

Even more, this program offers a different view of pathways to global transformation and a truly new world order. It is not about change that comes from the top down. Nor is it about horizontal shifts of power from one state or bloc to another. It is about global transformation from the bottom up and inside out. It is about governance from within. It is about a transformation of souls. As David Wick, a leader in the movement for a global culture of peace has noted,

> "This is about shifting mindset and behavior in all aspects of our societies as we move from force to reason, from conflict and violence to dialogue and peace-building, and embrace humanity's interconnectedness and inner oneness."

As such, this program sets new benchmarks for the human journey into a multicultural world community. At the time this program was rising through civil society and UN circles, the existing world order was going through significant change. The Cold War was ending. Analyses by Samuel Huntington and others asserted that the bipolar world order dominated by superpowers was now giving way to a multipolar world in which there would be increasing conflicts between major world cultures or civilizations.

Cultures and cultural identities are not contained neatly within the borders of nation states, but cross and transcend them. Cultural identities are shaped by beliefs, ideologies, histories, and networks that function globally and regionally as well as locally. A state-centric world system is not adequate to address a potential "clash of civilizations."

Five decades before Huntington's analysis, the historian Arnold Toynbee had written extensively on the rise and fall of civilizations. Toynbee's work underscored the importance of religion and spirituality in the rise of civilizations. Civilizations that lost their spiritual core died from within. New cultures and civilizations arose from the ashes of the old through a creative minority with a new spiritual vision. One reason that cultures and the religions and beliefs that shape them are key to peace is that they carry the symbols, archetypes, meanings, and deep identities of a people. Political and economic arrangements are superficial in comparison. Cultures go to the deep core of a people's sense of identity and the meaning of what it is to be human and a human community. Cultural identities also shape patterns of cohesion, disintegration, and conflict formation.

Toynbee saw the long arc of future history leading toward world unity and a global civilization. But on the journey toward that end, he also saw the potential for a collision of cultures, with successive waves of violence and counter-violence. To prevent this, he urged religions and cultures to let go of their hostilities and engage in inter-religious and intercultural dialogue for the purpose of finding common ground. This intercultural dialogue would be key to war prevention and peace building.

Toynbee's proposal was not mere wishful thinking. In fact, inter-religious dialogue and ecumenism had already been growing beginning in the early 20th century when he was writing. Parallel with the League of Nations and the United Nations religious networks were seeking ways to overcome their role in past wars and find common ground for their role in building world peace. The common ground sought was not just religious, but often focused on the same global agenda being addressed by the UN. Increasingly, these international religious groups worked interactively and, eventually for some, in partnership, with the UN and its programs.

Secular international non-governmental organizations in growing numbers, with members from diverse cultures, also played a growing role in addressing global issues. According to the Union of International Associations, there were 176 international nongovernmental associations in 1909. By 1985 that number had multiplied to more than 18,000, and by 2022 to 41,000. Many of these organizations link with the UN and its specialized agencies and programs in collaborative efforts to address human concerns ranging from education, environmental protection, economic development, human rights, refugees, child-welfare, the status of women, intercultural dialog, and other forms of peace building. This global civic society is playing a vital role in shaping a more peaceful and humane future. "We the peoples" are not just objects of governmental decisions and actions. We are also agents of social change, with shared care and responsibility for the world's future.

Government may offer a vision and official support but cannot conjoin the hearts and minds of disparate and conflicting peoples into a "We the People." The people themselves must embark on a journey to bridge divisions and transform attitudes; to encounter, engage, and become open to one another; to discover, affirm, and bond with one another. To become an inclusive world community, a thousand dividing lines must be bridged. Governments alone cannot build all the bridges. "We the peoples" must also build bridges and personally journey across economic, cultural, religious, racial and attitudinal divides.

The bridge work is still underway. Old fractures and scars are still being healed. But a journey is a process and those who enter a cross-cultural process discover not only the "other" but also themselves. They can grow into their own humanity and become more fully themselves.

Garfield Vernon's account describes his journey within this larger context of the world journey. His journey took him into homes of people of diverse cultures, into world conferences and into the corridors and offices of the United Nations where he was engaged with decision makers. Along the way he was inspired and supported by fellow travelers. He was nurtured by ideas in the books he read and by mentors in his home, school, and life. The going was not always easy. He met obstacles but got up, tried again, and went deeper. In the process of that journey, of opening to "the other" and "otherness," he found a deeper appreciation for his own culture and identity as well as of others.

Each person's journey is at once both personal and collective. Details about how different people experience and interpret another culture may vary. For example, my own journey growing up among farmers and factory workers of diverse faiths in the US Midwest would not at all lead me to conclude that the US is a culture motivated by profit. I cannot recall a single person that I would characterize this way. What I did see were diverse people who went to different places of worship and work, but who all seemed centered on God, family, and community. Nevertheless, I was fascinated to learn how Dr. Vernon experienced American culture.

There are thousands of stories to be told. No one can take this journey for others. In a way it is a solo trip. But we can share our stories and guide one another. *Toward Cultural Intelligence* invites us to find ways to turn fear of the other into understanding and enrichment. Ultimately all our personal journeys flow into the collective journey, the story of humanity struggling, and hopefully learning, to affirm diversity and to live together within one Earth home. Welcome aboard. It may be a rocky, but nevertheless a rewarding and an unforgettable, journey.

Toward Cultural Intelligence

A Personal Journey
In New Perspectives
For Achieving Global Peace

Introduction

Ever since childhood, I have had a lifelong interest in human cultures, how they differ, and how and why some harmonize so well, while others do not. Alongside that fascination developed a burning passion for peace, for understanding what fosters peace, what advances it, what obstructs it.

What does foster peace? What makes it possible and viable? Answers vary, and to be sure there is no one single factor.

But the principal answer is something I have come to think of as cultural harmony. Yes, world peace has its heroes and its martyrs—the Gandhi's, the Martin Luther Kings. But in the end, peace is not a matter of single heroic individuals, or of written documents and paperwork agreements between states. Genuine peace is a relationship between cultures.

We have been told that the world is a place of competition and struggle, that in the battle that is 'the survival of the fittest,' some must lose for others to win.

But is that true? Cooperation is as much a reality as competition, and there is surely more mutual benefit in mutual support than in constant collision.

Nature does not greet us only with images of conflict. No less present is a phenomenon called symbiosis: "an interaction between two different organisms living in close physical association, typically to the advantage of both."

As in nature, so in human nature: all around us is the possibility of cultural symbiosis, an interaction between cultures that enriches and enhances both, and that is the genuine basis for peace. For true peace involves one community of people learning to think of other communities of people with respect and acceptance; learning to appreciate others rather than demonizing them and learning to do so without depreciating or effacing their own culture.

How is that harmony achieved? Through a process of cultural competence. It is truly amazing and wonderful to see that at certain times and places, and in certain people, this competence has come about naturally.

But such accidental competence is the exception. Building that fragile harmony consistently and universally requires a fluidity and skill; a skill that must be cultivated through education and training.

The need for those skills has never been greater. After the fall of the Soviet Union, the American writer Francis Fukuyama famously announced, "The End of History." There was now one superpower, America, he asserted, and its successful system of liberal democracy and neoliberal capitalism would soon replicate across the earth. World cultures would reflect the new unipolar

American world economy and become mirror images of each other. Polarization would vanish. The world would finally be made safe for democracy, or at the very least McDonalds.

History did not end, and polarization did not happen. Polarization has exploded. As I write, there is talk of war between the Russians and the Ukrainians, war between the Chinese and the Americans, war even between the Americans and themselves. Newspapers spread the violent rhetoric of political dissent and rumors of civil unrest. Walls have gone up and supply chains broken down as nations block travel and shut down businesses because of the worldwide COVID-19 pandemic. Riots and protests take place in the streets, terrorist incidents multiply. In the words of Yeats:

Things fall apart; the centre cannot hold;
Mere anarchy is loosed upon the world,
The blood-dimmed tide is loosed, and everywhere
The ceremony of innocence is drowned

I contend that these things are not necessary. Peace is possible. Cultural harmony is attainable. Social perfection may never be fully realized, but social improvement can be furthered in a thousand ways. Societies, like individuals, can be a little better tomorrow than they are today, and if those small improvements are regular and consistent, massive progress can be made.

What it requires, however, are new tools and new approaches. Clearly the existing ones are not working.

But where do we find these new tools? What sorts of new tools are they?

What kinds of new approaches? And why have things changed so drastically during the past few decades? How and why has our social situation become so negatively transformed?

This book doesn't contain all the answers. But I do believe that it points out directions where those new tools can be found and forged.

In a 1963 article in the Journal of the American Psychoanalytic Association, Dr. K. R. Eisler discussed the idea of a 'psychoanalysis of history,' and suggested that the history of groups (specifically, nations) could be regarded as, and treated, as though they were the history of an individual.

A good deal of time has passed since 1963, and psychoanalysis is no longer widely regarded as a highly effective tool for change. But newer and stronger therapeutic techniques have evolved, and data show that many of the techniques in that armory are extremely effective in producing change.

A culture is not quite the same thing as a nation, or a 'group,' but it is near enough for many of those techniques to be fruitfully adapted and applied.

Central to many of the most divisive conflicts the world faces today is the problem of cultural dis-harmony. The customary way of dealing with it has been to ignore the problem, and to hope that, over many generations, integration or assimilation will take place. In some cases, it has. In other cases, millennia have passed, and discord has only worsened.

These problems have been addressed by spending trillions on social programs, or on marketing propaganda, or through the application of increasingly totalitarian political pressure. Occasionally these have had some small and brief success. But mostly have ended up in failure.

These combinations of inaction and manipulation have failed because they ignore the lived, existential dimension of the populations they address: their psychologies—their minds and spirits. These approaches have been culturally incompetent because they view cultures as objects to be re-shaped rather than as living entities, as collectives of people to whom a sympathetic friend must listen, and empathize, before assistance can be rendered.

Today's therapies provide exactly the tools, tested successfully in practice, that, adapted, can foster the cultural competence that is needed to provide lasting positive change.

These tools and approaches are not simply lying there. A great deal of research and study are needed to distinguish the most effective therapeutic tools and determine which are effective when applied to culture. Still further research and creativity are needed to modify and adapt such techniques to cultures and cultural interaction. I can only sketch the general outlines of a cultural therapy here, and hope that the idea finds support.

But—in a world that is increasingly more and more divided—I feel that no area shows more promise, and no effort is more justified, gives more hope, or is worthy of more support.

Even before we can begin, however, aspiring cultural therapists must reckon with a challenge never seen in history or in human society—a social development that I have come to regard as key to understanding the cultural changes of the day.

That development is the internet.

Why did History not end? Why has the division between peoples worsened in recent years?

I believe much of the answer can be attributed to the new digital environment in which we are all immersed. We live now in two worlds: the everyday world of real life, the world of our physical surroundings; and a second life online where we interact with others and present a personal and cultural image to the world.

Initially there was no notion that a 'culture of the internet' would evolve. It was felt that this new mode of communication was simply a quicker way of passing messages to one another. The internet was even naively welcomed as a path leading to closer communication between cultures—as the arrival of a world forum into which all nations would contribute and share their thoughts, and from which a single global community would eventually emerge.

Again, that has not been the case. As recent years have shown, there are few things in the modern world that foster cultural division more.

It is not simply that social media sites abound in hate speech, or that terrorists have been as ready to use the internet as diplomats. The true problem lies with an online cultural fragmentation, a strange and unexpected form of mental self-segregation that mimics culture but exaggerates and debases it. In essence, this stems from the commercially driven fact that intelligent search engines increasingly tell us only what we want to hear, and that the relationships we form online are increasingly only with people who think like us.

Advertisers have learned that it is profitable to serve up the familiar and that which provides immediate gratification. And so, increasingly the internet drives people into closed online cultural communities. Like a turtle drawing itself into an impenetrable shell, users isolate and insulate themselves, experiencing the world and other cultures through a set of biased images rather than direct experience.

I am by no means advocating a Luddite withdrawal from this technology. On the contrary. There is no better way to access needed information, or to spread it. What is happening, however, is that as people withdraw into such informational cocoons, such digital echo chambers, the only cultures they encounter are their own. And not even really their own, but a simplified, inorganic, and increasingly paranoid and abrasive substitute.

The tendency of these online subcultures to radicalize is now well known. What is less well understood is their tendency to distort and characterize the underlying, genuine, culture of the user. The pandemic has only accelerated this digital self-segregation, as people interact less and less with the real world and more and more with images passing across their screen.

Cultures are no longer merely themselves, but are accompanied by a cultural shadow, an online reflection in which the original culture is expressed in distorted ways. That distorted reflection seeps into and distorts the original underlying culture itself. The living culture begins to resemble what it only appears to be.

There may well be ways that such online expressions

of culture can enhance the underlying culture. There may well be ways that such expressions can enhance cultural symbiosis. So far, the record has been mixed, and a good deal of study is needed before we know more. A significant part of this book is devoted to just this question.

We are, in short, in a period of great crisis. New challenges face us, and new tools are needed to deal with these contemporary issues and new landscapes. I believe that certain core concepts I have been developing—the notions of cultural shadows, cultural therapy, and existential multiculturalism—can foster greater cultural intelligence, which can provide more helpful tools and guidelines for an era in much need of such help. Much more research will be needed, but every journey begins with a destination and a direction. That direction is a step back from the painful cultural divisions that have disfigured human history, and a step forward towards peace.

Although these are large and abstract subjects, I have striven to make this book actionable. But, given the novelty of some of the concepts, I have chosen to elaborate them through a somewhat autobiographical framework. I want to show how these ideas came about through the course of my personal experiences, and what inspired them.

The world can be made better, and the people in it can learn to get along better. The goal seems so simple! And in many ways, it is.

But it involves an element that I touch upon by the book's end—the spiritual, religious, *existential* element.

One does not have to belong to any religion to increase one's cultural competence. But I have found that to genuinely work toward peace and foster cultural harmony, what is needed is an existential spark, an inner commitment. To build peace without, we must first find peace within. A love for other cultures begins with love itself, just as coming to regard others as one's siblings begins with realizing that we have a common Parent.

It is said that we must be the change that we want to see in the world.

That, I think, is the foundation stone of every attempt to cherish and aid all human cultures, and to further human culture as such.

We must begin with *passion*. We must begin with ourselves.

Part One

A
Personal
Journey

Chapter One

A
Multicultural
Boyhood

A Multicultural Boyhood

We are all born in a particular time and place. We are all born to parents with a unique heritage, and in a community with a history and customs all its own. We come into this world as a part of a people, a people who have their own unique identity, their own ways of living and acting and worship, and who have their own way of relating to other groups of people.

As newborn children we are blissfully unaware of this. We are born into a world that is all the world we know, and in our earliest years we pay no attention to it—we simply accept it and live in it, joyously and unreflectively, the way newborn birds fly freely through the air.

When I think about my childhood, I return to that feeling, that acceptance, because I have had a lifelong interest in human cultures and how they can relate peacefully to one another. I have read hundreds of books and articles on the subject, attended classes and conferences and seminars on the subject, written a dissertation involving the subject, worked, and striven for it, and yet sometimes I think I have never been closer to the lived experience of multicultural acceptance and peace than as a child.

"The end of all our exploring," wrote T. S. Eliot, "will be to arrive where we began and to know the place for the first time." How true that is. It sometimes seems to me that all my studies have been a way to return to those first wonderful experiences of peace, acceptance, and tolerance.

It is strange how so many things that are difficult and complex for adults are clear and simple to children. As a child I accepted my culture and the fact of other cultures easily and naturally, without reflection. One Jamaican neighbor might be black, another white, another Chinese, another Indian or British—that was simply how things were. Tourists might come from any nation in the world and speak any language. Each would look and dress and act in their own way. That was simply how they were, and it was fine—all these people coming and going were interesting, not threatening. A pleasure to see, not a burden to shun. Acceptance and tolerance were natural.

Looking back, I now understand that it wasn't a matter of pure chance.

Jamaica is a culture whose economy very much depends on tourism. Welcoming travelers from different countries is how many Jamaicans make their living. It was the beginning seed of a later insight—that cultures could harmonize best when each offered the other some mutual benefit.

But I was a child: I was living, not analyzing. All I knew was that in general there was a welcoming feeling, a genuine openness. It was not a surface matter, not cool politeness. It had emotional depth. And the depth of Jamaican emotions was not always a good thing. One of the things that shocked me even as a child, and that shocks me still, was the rudeness that would sometimes erupt among Jamaicans. Jamaicans are not all angels. A crassness and a violence simply burst out of people at times.

But when it happened, it was individual not ethnic, personal not cultural, within different groups rather than between them. And they were exceptions so rare that as a child I barely noticed them.

Overall, I cherished my good fortune. I was lucky. Blessed! I was born in Jamaica, a nation vivid with many cultures, many faiths, many peoples, a nation that is uniquely open and tolerant of different ways of life. For Jamaicans, multiculturalism is not a goal—it's a lived reality, a celebrated reality.

Why? That is a puzzle I have spent my life trying to solve—the puzzle of why different cultures who have every reason to live in harmony with each other instead harbor an enduring collective loathing, and animosity that breaks time and again into hatred and violence; the puzzle of why, despite all the wisdom and benefits of peace, people time and again chose conflict and war.

But that is not a puzzle that absorbed me as I child. It didn't come to my attention then because everyone around me seemed to get along. Tolerance was not an ideal but simply a fact, a life-giving fact like the air that I breathed.

In retrospect I think part of the explanation was the sheer natural wonder of Jamaica. The Russian novelist Dostoyevsky once said, simply, "Beauty will save the world." Nowhere have I seen beauty in more abundance than in Jamaica. The blue depth of its skies, the crystalline infinity of its surrounding sea, the green gardens, the blue lagoons, the soft breezes, the whisper of the tides lapping the shores. To witness these things is to be elevated, to be hypnotized.

You cannot be intoxicated by both beauty and hatred at the same time. Who can hate, when it's so easy to lie on the beach with someone you love instead?

I was born in a rural district, Silent Hill, near the town of Christiana.

Most people there remain heavily dependent on agricultural activities for subsistence. It lay in the parish (the equivalent for a State or Province) of Manchester and is a tropical countryside with lush greenery. No child could ask for more exhilarating landscapes. I truly believe that the pure loveliness of the surroundings is part of the reason for our great Jamaican tolerance.

Another reason, perhaps, is the central role of family and faith in Jamaica. That was certainly the case with my parents, Sylvester and Jean. Somehow, they had picked up the nicknames Guy (for my father) and Pat (my mother's nickname). My father was a police officer, and at that time my mother had been a teacher, which is probably why my own later entry into the world of education was so smooth and almost inevitable. I had an older sister, Maxine, and a younger brother Dwayne, but the one message they drilled into all three of us, constantly, was one of respect—respect for other people, other cultures, other ways of life, and other ways of thinking. Every other family we knew did the same. Woe to the child that referred to anyone with a racial or ethnic slur! Parents would correct them, generally with a switch, quickly and in no uncertain terms.

It was doubly so in our household. My father and mother might only be humble civil servants in a small rural community, but they were intelligent, sophisticated and well-informed individuals. They made it very clear to me that education was the most important attainment of all, and education was above all an exposure to an ongoing world of differences: the great writers and thinkers and people of history were, to my parents, members in a chorus of voices whose conflicts bore an inner harmony: each were travelers taking their own best route to truth.

I learned to regard these great historical voices this way almost without reflection, for this was the way my parents regarded them, and my parents were my model: their behavior was wise and natural. Other families might not be as fortunate, but in Jamaica this core value of tolerance and respect for others was universally shared. Eventually I came to see the role of family as central. We imagine peace and cultural tolerance to be matters discussed at conferences and official gatherings, but, in truth, it is at our parents' tables that these core attitudes are formed.

And—in my case, at least—that formation was a delight. When your mother is an educator, and both your parents esteem knowledge and learning, you find yourself attending school almost from the moment of birth. Academic subjects, reasoned arguments, fine language, the issues of the day and the history of yesteryear, are topics of everyday conversation that surround you even before you can understand them. I loved my parents with all my heart, but they were not simply parents—they were interesting. They knew all sorts of things.

I remember once laughing when I read how an American writer described his father's answer to a question: "Shut up,' he explained."

That was never the response of my father, or my mother. They encouraged every hint of curiosity in their children: our educations began from the moment we could stand. For me, kindergarten was post-graduate instruction.

I did eventually have to go to school, alas. I was sure I would never be able to learn as much at school as I could at home. But my parents said that part of the value of going to school was to meet and socialize with others, and, like all Jamaicans, I had very positive feelings about others. Even at Silent Hill, I often played with other children from different cultures. Or perhaps I should say somewhat different cultures. There were Chinese and other Asians, and children whose families came from continental India, but nearly all of them were born and raised in the same rural environment.

They were Chinese or Japanese or Indian Jamaicans.

When the time came to go to school, however, I began to encounter and interact every day with children and adults freshly arrived from Europe and North America. They were different. They were not tourists or passersby or naturalized Jamaicans.

For the most part the adults were missionaries, here to preach the word of God. But they did a good deal more than that, and we Jamaicans very much appreciated it and welcomed them. They provided health care at medical missions, assisted at schools and hospitals, and taught classes in a whole range of subjects to children and young people and even adults. It's rather common nowadays to dismiss missionaries, especially the European ones, as 'imperial colonizers,' but that did not remotely describe the genuine contribution these people made, not the kindness and idealism which drove them to make it.

The middle and high school I went to was founded and initially led by a Scottish Presbyterian. Over time, native Jamaicans increasingly filled the staff and teaching posts, but a few Scots remained, and their Scottish heritage seemed to tinge everything about them from the way they dressed and held themselves to the way they spoke English. Not for them Jamaican Creole or Rastafarian English! Nor did they sound like the Beatles on the radio, or John Wayne in the films. I shake my head sometimes when I hear people talk about 'white people' as though Scots and American cowboys and French chefs are all one and the same. No! All soup is soup, but not all soups have the same flavor.

Did I think of them as belonging to a different 'culture'? Not yet. But one Scottish missionary was to change all that. For I was blessed by having a Scottish debate trainer whose memory I honor to this day. Her name was Helen R. Stills. She was one of the principal educators at the school, and I have never had a better teacher or a more inspiring professional. What a powerful, imposing figure she was—perhaps six feet, strong and commanding. Like a great bear, she was heavy-set physically, and towered over me.

But she seemed to sense that I had a natural gift for

speaking, and for some reason became determined to polish this small rough stone of a young boy into the gleaming diamond of a fine orator. After my classes I would often be summoned to her office to be drilled in elocution. But not just elocution. Erudition! Mrs. Stills would fly over a whole range of topics and matters, ideas, and history. Socrates and Dickens, Saint Paul and Robespierre, Gandhi, and Lenin! Dueling with her during our conversations, for the first time I became intoxicated with the spark and fire of ideas.

Here I was, a young Jamaican boy of 11 years old, and there she was, a white woman and a Christian missionary, but somehow, falling into the pure river of eloquent language, we met in a common love of vivid and intelligent thought and expression. I would quote Shakespeare; she would respond with a great avalanche of Shaw and Carlyle. I would cite Caesar, she would counter-attack with Cicero. Such a fluid and dynamic exchange! And it was an exchange, and an equal exchange: I stood up for my opinions as rigorously as she stood up for hers. "Maybe you think you should be sitting in this seat," she once sniffed at me from behind her scholarly desk as I forcefully made my case.

Truly, I thought that would be a fine and honorable place to be. Perhaps my academic aspirations began that moment.

Our talks were not always the lively cut and thrust of debate, far from it.

Sometimes she would reminisce about Scotland and its people so vividly that I felt I knew them. And what experiences she had known—World War One, World War Two, revolutions, depressions, a passing of epochs.

Yet underlying it all was a persistence of deep spiritual mission.

I had other speech trainers, and very fine ones, but she had a special quality, a quality that spoke to me and opened much of history and English literature for me. More than that: insights into the English and European mentality.

And even more than that: for it was in those classes and in those discussions that I first began not merely to live but to truly grasp the idea of culture.

There in Jamaica, as a young boy, I knew Chinese and Indians, Europeans and Africans, tourists from every country and expatriates with none. There was white and there was black, but no one seemed to care very much. It was just how things were. People lived the way they chose and got on well with one another. Yes, I was seeing things from a child's perspective, but what I saw was sensible and good. It was a social fact but not a social problem.

Schooling changed all that. Life in Jamaica might be tolerant and peaceful, but life outside, as recorded throughout history, was pure nightmare. Genocide! Slavery! Imperialism, violence, race riots, oppression, colonization, Inquisitions, servitude, ethnic conflict, brutality. The suffering generated by intolerance was jaw-dropping in its scope and intensity.

I had taken peace and tolerance for granted. I had no idea that, historically, these were the exception, not the rule. I had not thought of these things as conditions that needed to be fought for and established. Now, as I read about figures like Gandhi and organizations like the League of Nations and the United Nations, I began to see how great and important was the effort to build some measure of harmony between all these contending actors—these contending cultures. "Blessed are the peacemakers," said Christ during the Sermon on the Mount, and nothing proved his words truer than those moments in history when they were momentarily forgotten.

Some figures, it seemed, could rise above that, and I began to focus my studies there. Why did some cultures harmonize so well, and others not at all? Why did they resolve their issues in some cases, and collapse into war and conflict in others? What structures could be put in place to foster peace and harmony? What could one single person do? Some of my fellow students found all this silly. Go dance, Garfield, relax, play soccer. Stop asking the impractical questions of a dreamer and idealist.

Was I a dreamer and an idealist? If so, I was proud of dreams and my idealism!

Others around me were not so indifferent—there were some capable of embracing other cultures, not rejecting them. Mrs. Stills, for instance. My growing curiosity about the world beyond Jamaica, was matched by Mrs. Stills' love for Jamaica. In time I believe she became a naturalized Jamaican citizen. I know that eventually she retired in Jamaica, and passed away there.

But she and her tough Presbyterian Christianity, the sheer sweep of her learning and her personal integrity, added even more weight to the impression she made, left on this student an indelible mark. I was not the only person she left deeply impressed: in time she became the President of the Jamaica Teachers' Association.

I was also very much taken by the Chaplain of my

school, another Scot, a gentleman by the name of the Reverend John Purves. He was not so physically imposing as Mrs. Stills, but he had the same spiritual strength and the same natural, almost casual, eloquence. I admired them greatly, not least because, through their deep and sincere religious faith, they seemed to point beyond themselves to something greater than themselves. I loved my native Jamaican culture, of course, and I loved the easy tolerance with which it welcomed others so easily, but these two teachers showed me how easily one could love, genuinely love, other traditions and cultures too, all without giving up one's natural affection for home and one's heritage in the least. Inspirational teachers such as these proved priceless to my development: they taught me how to say *Viva La Difference* with all my heart.

And between the two of them—and along with my parents—they had quietly shaped my cultural curiosity and desire for exploring and navigating thresholds of cultural differences.

I felt naturally at home in academia. I loved to study, I loved the depth and battle of ideas. Just as some people are born athletes, naturally fitted for the life of the body, some are naturally fitted for a life of the mind.

Finding out more about another person's culture came easily to me.

But I wanted more than that. Mrs. Stills and the other teachers had opened my eyes up not simply to history and ideas, but to our moral responsibility to the rest of the world. I did not want to bury myself in a cocoon of books when so many people in the world were struggling and suffering, persecuting and being persecuted.

It might be only as a naive child, but here in Jamaica

I had tasted the reality of cultural harmony. The horrific cultural conflicts elsewhere which I learned about in my studies appalled me. I wanted to end it, or, at the very least, to minimize it to whatever small extent I could. I had begun to find a focus to my life, a subject to which I could devote my studies, a goal to which I could devote my career: Cultural harmony. Peace.

I would deepen that study in institutions of higher education. But the immediate next step in my journey was to experience in real life what I had so far only encountered in books—to travel and experience the reality of other cultures in the disruptive world of today.

Chapter Two

Seeing
The
World

Seeing The World

As time passed, I went on to study at other institutions of higher learning. There, I was once again blessed with an undergraduate professor of tremendous integrity and brilliance. His name was Dr. Lewin Williams and more than anyone else he introduced me to the intellectual dimensions—and the often-brutal reality—of culture and history in the modern world.

It was a sobering transition from Mrs. Stills. For all her learning and intelligence, Mrs. Stills remained wed to a sort of romantic historiography. She was a Christian, as was I, and since Christianity was born in the classical world, the intellectual dimensions of her world retained something of those limits. We might discuss Plato and Aristotle, Seneca and Augustine, Calvin and Luther, and argue about them thoroughly, but we did not discuss the thought of Mao or Foucault. The modern world of materialism and atheism was not to her taste. She regarded the American Founding Fathers as the last of the classical thinkers. After that? *Le Déluge*. When Robespierre displaced classical and Christian statures and put the

Goddess of Reason in their place, they had crossed a line into a realm Mrs. Stills did not wish to follow—the realm of the totalitarian ideologies of Second World, which she remembered with little joy.

Professor Williams, on the other hand, knew the modern world and its ideas intimately, and presented them masterfully. And what a feast of ideas it was! It was Dr. Williams who first opened my eyes to the gigantic ideologies of Marxism-Leninism. That is not to say that he was himself a Marxist; he was not. Nor is it to say that we agreed about the material he presented. If anything, our discussions, and debates, in class and out, were even more far-ranging and intense than my frequent contests with Mrs. Stills.

But Dr. Williams helped me to see how intensely figures like Marx had struggled to make sense of the modern world: to grasp its mechanics in all their profound fullness of detail, and to try to use that understanding to contextually and appropriately re-shape society into something better. "Philosophers have only interpreted the world in various ways," wrote Marx. "The point, however, is to change it." I understood that point, but I wasn't sure I agreed. How can you change what you don't first understand? I nonetheless felt the noble and anguished intention behind it, the ache for a better world, and the intention was inspiring.

The actual history of Communism, however, was less so. Professor Williams was not blind to the Gulag or the Cultural Revolution, or the cost in lives they entailed. As such, he helped me see the difference between Communism as a revolutionary ideology, as a historical reality, and Marxism as a set of analytic tools, a method of sociological analysis. A Marxist perspective allowed you to clearly see the impact of economic factors on daily life and everyday culture. It helped you discern the reality of class distinctions, the clash of social opposition, and the sad dance of class struggle.

Such discernment was valuable. But I did not think that the solution to the problems that Marxist analysis revealed was an interim period of absolute dictatorship. As history showed, such an interim could last a very long time indeed. I came to think of Marxism as a Swiss Army knife: a useful set of sharp tools that could all too easily cut off your fingers.

This was still the time of the Cold War. For all the professions of friendship from the Americans, the USSR, and the Chinese, many in Jamaica felt that their nation was viewed by these lumbering superpowers as only another pawn on the chessboard. America might offer aid, the USSR seek an alliance, China offer to send advisors, but to many of us in the so-called 'Third World,' these were not gestures of heartfelt friendship so much as seductive recruitments into a global power struggle of which we wanted no part.

Maintaining a safe distance, however, was not really an option.

Propaganda and foreign aid from all these various players slowly began to foster a certain paranoia, both in the schools and among the learned elite. One side opted for Freedom (the United States), another for Socialism (the USSR), another for Revolution (Maoism).

I was for Freedom. But I found the thinking of the other sides well worth my attention. And I was struck by what I perceived to be the deliberate manipulation of culture by all sides: the crude way media and marketing and money and other sorts of influence were being used to sway people into one or the other camp. I couldn't help but wonder if there might be better goals for such techniques, as well as more honest techniques.

I am giving the wrong impression very much if it seems that my introduction to university life was one long stream of red star arm patches and guerrilla training. Far from it. It was at least as much an introduction to dating and dancing. Especially dancing some of Jamaica's traditional dances: bruckins, dinki-mini, maypole, and quadrille! There too I had discovered a new and wonderful area for exploring culture. For there is nothing like letting your feet fly alongside others to feel a cultural bond. In the classroom I had begun to think of myself as a citizen of the world; on the dance floor, with the band soaring and the drums thrumming, I was all Jamaican.

Those university days were not one long party: the Cold War was still at the back of many people's minds, and there were crises enough to remind us that it could instantly become hot. But even then, it appeared to be ebbing, and there were many other topics and thinkers to address.

I was especially taken at the time with Marshall McLuhan. The Canadian theorist had become world famous for announcing that the world of nation-states was coming to an end, and that we were all on the verge of becoming a "Global Village." Television and radio and other electric media were connecting every home and every village, said McLuhan, and now whatever happened in the world happened to everyone everywhere all at once. For better or for worse, we were all merging into one vast electric post-literate township—one world, one people, one culture.

Well, perhaps that was not exactly what McLuhan was saying, but at the time it was what many of us wanted to believe he was saying. I too was caught up in what I thought was his vision of the entire world melting into a community of oneness—a wild, swirling, funky, harmonious oneness.

But I resisted it. University was a tremendous intellectual feast, but at some point, even the tastiest of feasts results in indigestion. I needed breaks, and sometimes I took them. I socialized, I took part in cultural dances and sports; I dove into book after book. But over time I began to give myself over to a personal mission: the study of cultures and how to transition them from animosity to cooperation, from division and aversion to mutual empathy.

It seemed such a simple problem—how can institutions and everyday individuals help two different groups of people get along better? Wasn't it just obvious that working with one another was better for everyone concerned than working against one another? Yet so far, my university studies seemed not to clarify any possible solutions, but only to unnecessarily complicate the question. The more I studied, the less I seemed to know.

What was a culture? When I went to a student club and listened to reggae, or moved my body to ska or mento, or ate Ackee (the national fruit of Jamaica), when I strolled through my home district visiting my relatives, I didn't need to formulate an answer. I knew what my culture was, what a culture as such was. I could feel it.

Yet when I sat in class, poring through long texts on anthropology, Patristic history, comparative religion, semiotics, cultural sociology, and even the first shoots of what are now called cultural studies or 'Theory,' I knew I was learning a lot; but I wanted to engage with the world, not watch it from a cold distance.

The world cooperated — or at least the world of the university. One day I was called to the President's office. It seemed my academic record was such that the university wanted to know if I were available to go on a cultural immersion trip! If I agreed, it would not be a very distant trip, hosted in Suriname, and I'd be away from Jamaica for three months.

The Immersion trip was to be centered around training, team building, and personal reflection, with a view to helping participants learn how to build healthy cross-cultural relationships while challenging us to think in new ways. It was under an Exchange Student agreement for colleges and universities within the Caribbean region and sponsored by the Caribbean Conference of Churches (CCC). I would be able to see and have a first-hand experience of the cultures of the student representatives that would be in attendance.

Was I interested?

No.

I was ecstatic!

Two Cultures

I can't begin to describe my excitement as I stepped onto the aircraft taking me to Suriname. I felt like Stanley and Livingstone rolled into one. I laughed at myself for my own enthusiasm. I kept telling myself that Suriname was just another Caribbean nation, probably very little different from Jamaica if at all. It would be no more, really, than going from one part of the island to the other. Nothing to get all upset about.

I tried to calm myself down, remind myself of my scholarly responsibilities. After all, I was an aspiring scientist of cultures. I would study, analyze, and fathom. I would set an example for future Exchange Students. I would make this trip the cornerstone of my many future books and lectures. I would…

As it turned out, I would just barely survive. At least, that is how I felt. Was it the water? The food? People in Suriname favor a kind of fish stew I had never tasted before. Did it contain a stomach virus? All I knew is that I stepped off the plane with all the élan of Neil Armstrong setting his foot on the surface of the moon; and by day's end I was lying in bed unsure of whether I would live to see the next day.

This is no reflection on the Surinamese, and especially not on the program hosts, who were as kind and doting as they could be. We met, exchanged greetings, and I looked around at the faces of the Surinamese people and listened to the lilt of their musical Creole, so like and yet so unlike Jamaican Creole. The island was green and lush, the sky blue, the air clear. Were I in good health, it would have made for a wonderful vacation.

I was not in good health. Whatever I had eaten or contracted struck me over the head like an iron pipe. Nearly all my allotted time in Suriname was spent shivering and vomiting. I had come to learn about culture and the human condition. All I was learning about was its frailty.

I exaggerate—although it is quite hard to exaggerate how very ill I felt. After a few days I had regained enough strength to stand and even to walk and tried to use what dwindling time I had left to explore what I could of Suriname. It made a mixed impression. I was greatly disheartened by the poverty. No, this was not Jamaica, with its partying and its clubs, its reggae and its flourishes. The Surinamese labored under truly harsh economic conditions.

And yet there was a kindness and tolerance, a mutual support among its peoples. I had come to Suriname to experience a different culture, but even with only a little time to explore, I soon found that Suriname harbored an entire wealth of different cultures—Catholics and Pentecostals, Hindus and Muslims, Chinese and Africans and Javanese, Indians, even Amerindians. Strangely, though European influence seemed in abundance, there were very few white Europeans—almost none. Most Surinamese (a little over a quarter, I later learned) were of Indian descent. Yet of the fourteen languages spoken in Suriname, the principal one being Dutch (with which I was quite unfamiliar) even though I saw no one who seemed to be remotely of Dutch descent.

Sick as I was, I began to find Suriname a bit fascinating. How did this unusual mixture of peoples come about? It was the very image of diversity. More than that: it was the very image of tolerance and acceptance. The poverty might be disheartening, but there was a friendliness emanating from the people and between the people I met. It was touching and uplifting. I would have liked to have stayed and studied it more—if I weren't consumed with thinking about returning home.

Under the influence of my recent university reading, I tried to look at Suriname through Marxist spectacles, but without much success. Like Jamaica, it seemed that many people from many parts of the world had passed through Suriname, and many of those who passed through had remained—enough, at any rate, to make up a culture at least as diverse as that of Jamaica.

Unlike Jamaica, however, there seemed to me no booming tourist industry to buoy the economy up. It puzzled me, for I knew there was a magnificent Amazonian Rain Forest in the South, and waterfalls and a Nature Reserve that was one of the glories of the region.

Suriname was not a manufacturing powerhouse. There were mines, and there was agriculture, and so what labor there was, was hard and physical. The United States was the principal buyer of Surinamese goods, but it was hard to see either a proletariat or a capitalist in the milling streets—only people working very hard to feed themselves and their families.

Still, there was a humane tone to the Surinamese. Underneath all their diversity, all their poverty, was a quiet radiance: they were at peace with one another, at peace with the world. As the time came for me to go, I was almost sorry.

Almost, for the thought of having some Jamaican-style broths believed to improve one's immune system and boost metabolism, instead of whatever toxic bacteria I had ingested, was impossible to refuse.

My travels were not yet over, however. There was

one more nation to visit, Guyana, after a brief layover at Trinidad.

The stop at Trinidad was disconcerting. I had no time at all to study the culture or explore conditions. But here the feeling of social tolerance that was so evident in Suriname had utterly faded. Most of the people I saw were either Indian or black, and there was a distinct coolness between the groups, and a certain self-segregation. It was not open animosity, but one could not escape its undertone.

Regrettably, that impression persisted as I entered Guyana. Even more regrettably, so did my nausea. Whatever had tied my stomach into a knot in Suriname had clearly accompanied me across borders.

Mercifully, it wasn't quite as hard-hitting this time. Again, my hosts were as gracious as they could possibly be, and what I was given to eat (or rather, what I could keep down) was thoughtfully bland. I wasn't entirely bedridden this time and could get around.

What I found in Guyana, however, was as much a puzzle as what I had seen in Suriname.

There was diversity too in Guyana, but there was also vivid division. It seemed to exist most intensely between the Indian population and the black population. The black population itself was divided into nine tribes, which were not all in harmonious accord either. But if anything united the tribes, it was aversion to the Indians. I do not want to give the impression that there was fighting in the streets; day-to-day life was peaceful enough. But it was not a peace of the spirit. It seemed forced, though I could see no enforcers beyond unspoken social rules.

Possibly it was simply the wake of an unfortunate history. Much of the population of Guyana had arrived as slaves. Even the bulk of the Indian population, I was told, had been brought there against their will under indentured servitude. Whatever the cause, there was an edge to Guyanese society that saddened me—even though it also intrigued me.

What accounted for it? Guyana was so like Suriname! Over forty percent of the people lived under the poverty line. Again, mining and agriculture were the twin pillars of working life. Again, the United States (and Canada) were the principal recipients of their exports. Again, the landscapes and waterfalls were glorious, with much of the world's biodiversity nestling gloriously in their rich fauna. Poverty aside, Guyana was by no means the worst place in the world to be.

Yet there was a clear internal rancor. Not only internal: Guyana seemed involved in a series of constant border disputes with its neighbors, Suriname and Venezuela.

This discomfort with 'the other' certainly did not extend to me. Each group of Guyanese I personally met were nothing if not kind and accommodating. The muted aggression I felt only seemed to spill out when it concerned their own internal peoples. And it was an ambiguous phenomenon: the Guyanese found a very positive outlet for it in sports, which was universally celebrated and followed. But it also appeared negatively, in the persecution of marginal groups.

I was particularly struck by two facts. On the one hand, Guyana had one of the highest literacy rates in the entire Caribbean, over 96%. On the other, the Guyanese

25

had the highest rate of suicide in the entire world.

But it was not hard to imagine that the quietly intolerant tolerance of the Guyanese could express itself in an aggression directed against oneself, too. Intolerance has a dark karma.

It was also rather sad to think that a literate and well-educated people would not be more accepting of each other's differences. But then I remembered Mrs. Stills, who had brought up the case of Germany many times in our debates as an example of a highly sophisticated and intellectual country that had given itself over to the demons of racial superiority and hatred. It was a lesson I had not forgotten. One needed to cultivate the heart, not only the head.

Perhaps I am being too critical of Guyana. People there did manage to live in peace with one another and with their neighbors. But the experience of both cultures left an impression on me that I would not be able to express in intellectual terms for several years—the sense that there is an emotional component to multiculturalism that most of its advocates and analysts ignore.

Where multiculturalism is concerned, time and again we hear the word hate. Hate speech, hate crimes, hate groups. It's as though world media spends all its time trying to associate the notion of cultural diversity with hate.

Where is love? Where is the joy that we take in other cultures, the pleasure that we enjoy in novel differences, the relish we feel when experiencing the fresh and new and exceptional?

As a student of culture, immersed in the scholarship of culture, I was becoming more and more adept at applying the accepted formulae and the usual measurements and the conventional analytical tools when describing and assessing other cultures; but even then, I was beginning to suspect that there was an element of feeling, of lived experience, that was being overlooked in so much supposed learning. There was a deeper way to connect with other cultures than the 'tolerance' of grudging endurance, and I knew that deeper connection would have to be made if genuine peace were ever to flourish.

But exactly what that deeper connection was, I did not then know. And I would not be able to search for it intelligently for quite a while.

I did not even know that my visits to Suriname and Guyana had begun to open that door for me just the tiniest crack.

But they had.

Cuba

Looking back today, I see my first two cultural immersion travels as genuine and valuable learning experiences.

I didn't see them that way then.

Then, I regarded my two visits as complete and utter disasters. I had gone out to see the world, and all I had done is vomit on it! I had spent most of my time lying flat on my back. I had hoped to be inspired by a first-hand experience of novel cultures, but all I had been inspired to do was to think about becoming vegetarian. What little time I had spent among people had left me with only quick fleeting personal impressions, useless as scholarly material.

"What did you observe about the local economic conditions, Garfield?" Professor Lewin Williams asked.

My stomach pains!

"What about the blood-sucking American Imperialists?" asked other students.

"What about the freedom-fighting Communist guerrillas in the hills?" asked still other students.

"What about the *girls!* Were they cute?" asked still others.

I brushed it all away. I had more important things to do—namely, sulk.

After a good solid day of brooding, though, I began to reflect.

If there were two things that I had learned from my visits—aside from remembering to bring my own water next time—it was that (a) things were not what I imagined they would be, and (b) Marxism did not describe what I saw very well.

The first was an understandable mistake, I suppose. I had been born and raised in a post-Colonial Caribbean nation with a good many natural wonders and a great deal of racial and religious multicultural diversity. I was traveling to two post-Colonial Caribbean nations with a good many natural wonders and a great deal of racial and religious multicultural diversity. I thought I would come across small but fascinating nuances that I could write about in my anthropology classes. I did not expect to see two very different societies relating to themselves and each other in strikingly different ways.

I thought that culture and cultural relations in Suriname and Guyana would pretty much resemble cultural relations in Jamaica. That was not the case.

But quite as much a surprise was that these very different societies seemed to have the same economic base, and that was a shock. It was a shock because it put into question certain basic sociological givens that, like so much in those days, were rooted in Karl Marx.

I don't want to give the wrong impression. Higher education in Jamaica has never remotely been a matter of Communist Party training. Students then and now were far more interested in Reggae than in Russia. But as a way of understanding how events were playing out in the world, Marxism provided many of us with the basic tools.

True, it was more a matter of crude suppositions we derived from Marxism than from high Marxist theory proper. We simply took it as a given that the rich exploited the poor, that socialism was better than capitalism, that socialism was inevitable, that the people should tell big business what to do and not the other way around. Part of Marxism's popularity too was that it presented itself as an alternative to the cruel history of Western colonialism and its exploitation of natural resources, not to say the human resource of slavery. Part was Communist support for Colonial independence. A support that had been supercharged by Mao and other Communist heretics.

Marx taught that history developed in accordance with immutable laws. One of these laws was that capitalist development had to be fully established before the next, proletarian, phase could emerge. Not many revolutionaries in Marx's time were happy with that thesis.

"What, we have to wait till capitalism takes over everything before we can do anything about it?"

Few revolutionaries are that patient.

Lenin changed all that. He argued—and demonstrated—that a revolutionary Communist Party could take political control of an undeveloped country and an undeveloped economy, and simply leapfrog over the capitalist phase, accelerating development by taking direct dictatorial control of the means of production and the workers. All it took was Party dictatorship—and sufficient terror.

The formula worked! The price in human suffering was immense, but Stalin did manage to drag Russia kicking and screaming to world superpower status in little more than a generation. Mao did lift China from British subordination to a status comparable to Russia just as quickly. And if the price was too high for some, new independent sorts of Communism were emerging— Titoism in Yugoslavia, for instance—which seemed to combine rapid economic progress without the need for large-scale terror.

The attraction of this new model for nations of the Caribbean, of Africa, of South America, should be obvious. No one really wanted to continue the Colonialist economic model. What good would that do, other than replace Western exploitation with local exploiters? A socialist model like that of Tito gave the Third World a blueprint for insurrection followed by rapid development that combined national independence while at the same time dispensing with the worst excesses of political terror.

It wasn't classical Marxism, and it wasn't exactly Leninism or Stalinism either, but it was an attractive mix! At least to some.

These new sorts of Communism, experiments like Yugoslavia and like Cuba, promised the benefits of rapid industrialization and modernization without the totalitarian pain. We could not go back into colonial capitalism, so going ahead into some sort of socialism seemed the only way forward.

The only question was—was it a way forward? Life under Stalinism wasn't. Even the Russians themselves admitted that. Was life under these new, novel, 'experimental' forms of Communism any better?

I didn't know. But I had seen three Caribbean nations whose 'economic base,' as Marx would put it, were extremely similar. And what I saw were three very different sorts of societies! It didn't seem to me that expropriating the grasping capitalist owners of Reggae clubs in Kingston, or Indian restaurants in Guyana, would have much of a positive effect on the people in those countries at all. I certainly didn't think that benevolent dictatorship would have a positive effect.

Yet this was what so many arguments at the University were all about in those days. I fell into them too. Personally, I leaned toward the Tito model of fairly libertarian socialism. But my trips to Suriname and Guyana put all this in question. I had made certain assumptions about those countries and how their economies influenced their cultures, and I had been proven wrong. Was I wrong about Marxism too?

I came to a conclusion that has since shaped much of my intellectual life: it wasn't enough to read about it, to talk about it. I had to see it, experience it.

And so, inspiration came to me. Why not go and have a look?

I approached Dr. Williams and a few others in the school administration and proposed a student trip—a trip to Cuba.

I pointed out the many worthwhile classroom discussions that would follow such a trip, its potential relevance to student understanding. Enough abstractions! Why not let a few of our students learn first-hand about the topics we were discussing, and report back their impressions?

There was a good deal of back and forth. Who would fund the trip?

Would the Cubans allow it? With what conditions would we have to comply? I continued to press away, pointing out the value to the students, the prestige of having the school send out these young cultural ambassadors.

I expected that probably nothing would come of it.

But to my surprise Dr. Williams called me in one day to tell me the good news.

The trip was on.

We were on our way to Cuba!

So what did I see in Cuba?

Exactly what I expected to see—the completely unexpected.

During the trip over, my mind was surging with contradictory images. Cuba was an island in the Caribbean Sea—no doubt it would be just like Jamaica. Cuba was Communist—either it would be a heavenly worker's utopia, or a hideous Gulag populated by chain gangs of slaves. Cuba was Latin American—surely there would be Sombreros and bull fighting and tortillas. Cuba was a foreign country—surely there was something in the water that would send me to the hospital.

Cuba was none of these things.

But what I did see amazed me.

For instance?

From the moment my foot touched the shore, and the guides appeared to greet us and take us to the hotel, I was astonished at the architecture.

Cuba's architecture! Where can I even begin? Cuba's architecture was an explosion of styles, a wild array of colors and materials and historical collages. There were entire blocks of apartments whose neoclassical facades were painted pink, yellow and robin's-egg blue in succession. One stepped into what one thought would be a restaurant and found oneself in a 19th-century French palace. Classical statues were everywhere, missing an arm here perhaps, or a head there, but a bas-relief of Greek Gods would soon draw your attention away from any blemish.

There were blemishes. Many magnificent buildings were in a strange sort of disrepair—corroded, but untouched by graffiti. Many magnificent buildings seemed entirely new. Not new in the sense of being those massive blocks of faceless concrete—properly classified by architectural scholars as 'brutalism'—that characterized Communist regimes elsewhere. I had my breath taken away by a post-Sixties Art School that was a village of circular brick-domed structures based on African huts!

Roman Courts, Renaissance villas, Art Deco, American Modern, corroded Gothic towers, walls covered in

Picasso-like surrealist mosaics— four centuries of every architectural style known to the West seemed to have been sprinkled liberally across Cuba like so much gourmet seasoning. Building after building was connected by long arcades, so that one could walk through them for miles without ever being burned by the sun.

I was stunned. For years I had read about and discussed and debated history. Now I felt as though I was literally walking through it era by era. It was intoxicating—too intoxicating. I felt as though I could spend months happily walking the streets without ever speaking to a single person.

But I wanted to speak to people. The buildings were astounding, and spoke volumes about Cuban taste, Cuban urban planning, Cuban openness to beauty, and even about Cuban tolerance of other cultures, if not their avid celebration of other cultures.

But buildings are not people. I was there to examine the living substance of the culture, not its dead (albeit magnificent) architectural expressions.

It was not difficult. Cafes were everywhere, people were friendly, and our guides seemed quite happy to sit down and take a break and savor a daiquiri off by themselves as we struck up conversations with local people. We would introduce ourselves to them as tourists, and patrons of the cafe seemed quite ready to chat. Were the conversations rehearsed, prepared for us beforehand? I didn't think so. We were teenagers, not spy material, and the chat was not invariably complimentary to the government.

No criticism was made of Castro, of course. But yes, supplies were sometimes hard to get. Yes, there was a black market, and the prices were outrageous. Yes, the Americans and their embargoes made life tough. But politics meant little to the Cubans I encountered. Possibly they avoided the subject of politics and economics because it was simply out of their hands. What was the point of talking about it? Their main interests lay elsewhere—the boxing matches, the soccer finals, the horse races.

Racial animosity, sectarian violence? What were those?

It occurred to me that there wasn't much racial animosity for the simple reason that most people appeared to be of mixed race to some degree or another. Nearly every family I had the pleasure to meet included mixed-race individuals. In manner they seemed rather more European than not, but more easy-going Southern European than stern Northern European.

Poverty? It was both immense and non-existent. No one had a lot of money, but on the other hand everyone had a ration book and had no worries about health care or housing. No one was homeless or slept in the street. No one (other than American tourists) flashed expensive watches or gaudy jewelry. Crime was not a problem. There was not much to steal, and I had the impression that the violent were dealt with promptly and violently. There was an egalitarian sense among those I talked to. No Cuban I met felt they belonged to a higher or lower class than any other Cuban. No Cuban aspired to any higher sort of level either—that competitiveness so characteristic of German or American entrepreneurs seemed absent, except in the national pastime: sports.

Was this, then, Communism? It was—to my surprise—strangely pleasant, and yet with an emphasis on strange, almost as though it wasn't Communism at all. I had seen it idealized so often, and vilified so often, that I was hard put to think of Cuba these laid-back easy-going people as Marxists at all, much less as an exporter of violent revolution. Everyone seemed not dissatisfied with Cuban life and didn't make a great deal of fuss about it. There was a certain *esprit de corps*, a definite patriotism, and a strong tendency to demonize America, though not Americans.

As far as culture went, white, black, or mixed-race, it was seamlessly and uniformly Cuban. It was not a multicultural society, but almost a post-multicultural one. The ingredients in the melting pot really seemed to have melted.

All the basics were being taken care of by the government. That might not amount to very much, but it was enough, and yet not enough to be worth fighting over. It seemed to leave Cubans curiously relaxed.

What was most unexpected was the way that Cuba made Communist society seem viable. At school and in my readings of history, Communism was always decked out in high stark drama. Revolution! Torture! War! Crisis! Cuba itself was nearly the spark for the closest humanity had ever come to full-scale nuclear war.

Yet looking across at the cafes with their flirtations and their Pina Coladas, it struck me that Cuban Communism was almost the exact opposite of so much highly touted bravura and hysteria—Cuba was relaxed, hazy, like a quiet buzz. Nothing very grand, but nothing very unpleasant either. Walking among the extraordinary historical buildings, I felt I had somehow come not to the cutting-edge vanguard of history, but to some point after the end of history, where there was nothing very much to do.

A Transcendental Humanity

I was wrong, of course. There was and is a great deal to do. Returning to Jamaica and to university life with all its abstract political discussions, its affected poses and verbal radicalism, I began to return as well to my earlier commitment, my decision to try to do some genuine actual good in the world. I had leavened my studies with a great deal of cultural theory and a little bit of cultural travel, but I knew that nothing I had done had actually improved the world in any way. Not by one jot or one iota.

It rankled. I wanted to make a difference, and I had not done a thing that in any way addressed the world's single greatest problem: the inability of its people to simply coexist in peace. All I had to do was open the newspaper, and there were Israelis fighting with Palestinians, China brutalizing Tibetans, tribal warfare in multiple African nations, rioting in American cities, wars, wars, and rumors of wars. What was to be done?

I began looking into charities and independent groups and NGO's, organizations like Amnesty International and Doctors Without Borders. Was it only that I was impatient, trying to do too much too soon? But then in my private reading one day, I came across these words: "If anyone saves a life, it shall be as though he had saved the lives of all mankind."

The lines spoke to me. Like any young romantic, I wanted to 'save all mankind.' Needless to say, that was beyond my powers, so what I did instead, despite all my intentions, was nothing.

But to free one political prisoner, feed one hungry child, bind one bleeding wound—that was something. Maybe it was something even I could manage to do.

By then I had grown up enough to realize that I could probably do it better in the company of others. Where could I find people with similar goals, and work with them?

On speaking about it with teachers and contacts at the university, and—once again—I found myself invited to travel. It seemed that there was an international conference being held in Switzerland. The formal title of the conference was World Moral Rearmament Conference, and it was being conducted under the auspices of the Initiatives of Change.

The goal was exactly the sort of thing I'd been thinking about—a meeting-place where those most committed to human betterment could go and connect with each other and brainstorm practical ways to make measurable improvements in the world. There were openings at the conference for students who wanted to include that in their way of life.

My school had put my name in as a national representative, and it was accepted.

Soon I would be on the road again.

I have always been an idealist. I have always had the utmost faith in humankind. I have always held the highest hopes for the human future. I have always dreamed of moral perfection. As a Christian, I have always dreamed of a community of Saints, and of the Kingdom of Heaven on Earth. I have always wanted to see these visions made flesh, to see these things realized and tangible, standing before me, real and living, in the here and now.

And I never have. I have never even seen them approached. Except once. When I attended that conference in Switzerland.

I know, I know—this is the language of a hyper-romantic, and no conference anywhere could be as powerful and moving as what I am about to describe.

But I am not merely describing the conference: I am describing the impact that it had on me. That impact that was life-transforming.

It took several minutes—hours, really—for me to realize what I was witnessing, but when I emerged from the shuttle into the wintry-like Swiss air and walked up the stairs and presented my invitation papers, I imagined that I would be seeing nothing more than a group of old men shuffling papers and making speeches and, like so many others, myself included, doing nothing.

Slowly I realized that it was not like that at all. I was seeing men and women of every race, every faith, every ethnicity and nation coming together with a common purpose, a common practical purpose: to propose, discuss, perfect, fund and implement an almost startling range of initiatives to do the very things I had been thinking about: feeding, sheltering, healing, reconciling, saving their fellow human beings.

Some participants wore burnooses, others burqas; some wore the collars of Anglican and Catholic priests, some wore native African dress; Japanese corporate leaders were there in meticulous Western dress, shaven-headed Buddhists appeared in yellow *kasaya* robes, and Orthodox prelates spoke under high miters and through long flowing beards.

They were all there with one purpose, one goal: to lift up suffering humanity, to take practical steps to help their fellow human beings live better lives.

These people—hundreds of them—had come together from every branch and variation of the human family to apply their intellect, their passion, their determination, for the betterment of the whole, to lighten the burden of the weakest and most lost among us. I understood their compassion, I saw the logic of their actions, and for a brief moment I felt that I was standing outside myself, witnessing the actions and the drama of something I have since come to think of as a transcendental humanity—a humanity in which people of every culture are cherished exactly as they are, cherish others exactly as they are, and work together as a dynamic collective to advance the best interests of each.

Yes, my reaction sounds extravagant. But having spent a lifetime of seeing and reading about people living indifferently, competitively, struggling to amass more for themselves and take from others, this sudden experience of witnessing an entire community dedicated to the collective good of all astounded me.

I saw now that this sort of life was possible; more, it was real. Not only was it real, but I was a part of it, I was a member of this community. I might only be a student, but I had experiences to share, suggestions to put forth, and a contribution to make, and I and my contribution were welcome. I too was giving my life to the betterment of the world, playing a part in helping others out of darkness and into light.

I was no longer in any doubt; I gave myself over to what I was seeing and to the global mission of this community, wholeheartedly.

And *did* we shuffle papers, and make plans, and attract funding? Did we do all the necessary unromantic things needed to push forward our very romantic goals? We did. It was a successful conference. It accomplished many of its goals. When it was over, people that otherwise might have been on the brink of war had taken a measurable step back from that brink. Dialogue had indeed displaced confrontation. Efforts were being made and funds and needed assistance were flowing to the injured places of the Earth. For a moment, the gravity of national estrangement had been suspended, and cooperation and unity had risen above it.

And so we exchanged cards and phone numbers, promised to connect again, and found our ways to taxis and returned to our homes. It was over.

But it also, truly, left me with a vision—a vision of a transcendent humanity, in which individual and community identity, collective tolerance and universal mutual support, lived and flourished in action and spirit, focused and dynamic and perfectly aligned. A vision of a life fully worth living.

For a moment I had walked into utopia, a genuine utopia that is open to all of us at any moment. The moment passed, but the memory never.

This was what I wanted my life to be.

Chapter Three

*Teaching
and
Thinking
About
Culture*

Teaching and Thinking About Culture

After Switzerland, my head was in the clouds for days. Weeks! I know: it sounds silly. In some ways I suppose it was. All I had seen were different men and women from all over the world come together to try to reduce international conflict, prevent wars, alleviate poverty, reduce persecution and discrimination. What was so exceptional about that? There were people like that in every country. I aspired to be one of them.

But perhaps that was why I was so taken with the Conference and its people. They were doing what I was only dreaming of doing. Moreover, they were doing it effectively, because they were a community of scholars and experts and key advisors, formulators of policy, ministers, industrialists, world and national leaders. They themselves were a new and extraordinary culture, a culture that I hoped might change the world culture outside the Conference in its own image. In their initiatives and discussions, I could see an entirely new kind of world community emerging.

Sadly, that world was not yet here. Problems outside

remained, and for all the voices calling for peace there were others outside still profiting from war and threatening violent chaos. All too many voices. Soon enough, in fact, the world was about to be plunged into another disastrous global conflict—but I will explore that in the next chapter.

Soon after I left the conference, so did my fellow attendees. As I witnessed from a distance their brief collective dissolving, my intoxication was replaced by a hard sobriety. Their convocation had served to accomplish at least some of the Conference's goals. What had all my recent travels accomplished? I had visited Suriname, Guyana, Cuba, Switzerland. I had been surprised, impressed, disappointed, and at the end inspired. But what had I done, other than watch and react individually and emotionally?

At Switzerland, as a guest and a student, I had assisted here and there and shared some of my thoughts. But In Switzerland, as in Suriname and Guyana and Cuba, I had for the most part remained on the sidelines as an observer.

Was my presence in any of the cultures I had visited genuinely helpful?

Seeing the figures at the Conference at their plans and negotiations and discussions, seeing them work across all their cultural differences to advance humane and rational goals, left me struck with an impression— the impression of intelligence.

Were my actions intelligent? I had been no more than a helpful observer, and proud to be of help. But their collective activity was not only reshaping the world but the way some of the leaders of the world were interacting with each other—reshaping society and individuals outside and in. School had taught me to observe, to think. But what exactly was I observing as I looked upon their collective action? What drove these activities, these attitudes, this cultural intelligence?

That last question, so casual and off-handed, began to haunt me. I was not even entirely sure what I was asking. I felt I was on the edge of a notion that was both complex and yet strangely simple.

After all, every one of us lives in a culture, and every one of our cultures interacts with other cultures. What was the best way of doing that, the best way of living in our own cultures yet interacting optimally with other cultures? How could we do that wisely? How could it be done globally? There were individuals acting across multiple cultures fluidly, effectively, binding cultures together to the greater benefit of both— people who clearly seemed to be able to deal with multiple cultures with greater intelligence than the xenophobes and the warmongers. What precisely were they doing, and how were they doing it? What was cultural intelligence?

Like all students, I kept a notebook. I wrote down the phrase, I made some rough formulations.

It seemed to me that cultural intelligence was first of all a matter of perception. A person with cultural intelligence actively strove to see other cultures, as well as his or her own, realistically. They were sober enough not to demonize or romanticize or exaggerate or misrepresent or distort 'the Other.' They tried to see things as they were. They might begin with misconceptions, but they corrected them.

A person with cultural intelligence was also suave, at ease: he or she could interact with other cultures comfortably, without being stilted or abrasive, without being offensive or easily taking offense. Their realism about other cultures (and their own) clarified the emotional sore points, the hidden assumptions, the deeper drivers underpinning different cultures, that needed to be handled gingerly. One could call it a natural diplomacy, but that word suggests formality. This was not a matter of pure form. Such people were visibly respectful, but it was more than that—they seemed to have a genuine interest in other people, other cultures.

Also, those with cultural intelligence did not manipulate. A person of high cultural intelligence did not see other cultures and their people as objects to be used or exploited or even transformed for the better without the consent of those people making up the culture. Such a person might share perspectives but would not impose them. They might suggest some trade or alliance for mutual benefit, but they would not forcibly take advantage of other cultures solely for their own benefit.

Later, in America, I would often hear a phrase used in negotiations: "Win-Win." I liked that phrase. It resonated with cultural intelligence. The culturally intelligent had a canniness for making their interactions with others positive and pleasant for all concerned. They invariably favored the carrot, never the stick.

As my list expanded, I noted that none of these qualities and practices needed to be excessive or overly emotional. "Love one another" was certainly a worthy ideal, but a person aspiring to cultural intelligence could begin with a great deal less. Simple politeness, for instance; a sensitivity to personal matters, a clear wish that the other flourish and be well, an eye to things held in common, generous support without undesirable interference—these were small things, but added together they produced a large, a transformative impact. "Do unto others as you would have them do unto you," was another timeworn yet timeless valuable principle. How would we ourselves like to be treated by those of other cultures? Clearly that suggested intelligent patterns to follow ourselves.

Of course, there was a vast deal of scholarly flesh to be added to these sketchy and rather sentimental bones. It was one thing to have an intuition, quite another to articulate it to the point that research could confirm or disconfirm one's ideas from a standpoint of general utility.

Still, I had seen it in Switzerland—that universal cultural respect and self-respect; that collective cooperation aimed at a concrete good for all human beings. It was not a dream or a mirage. I had seen competent people working together to put their high intelligence to a sublime use. I had seen it operating in front of my own eyes, the very opposite of the division and prejudice and violence that assaults us constantly in the streets and in the news. There was such a thing as a culture of tolerance and cooperation, a living community of charity and peace; a way, a path, of cultural intelligence. I had seen it. It was real.

I wanted to better understand that reality—I wanted to expand it, that others might share in it. It exemplified something I revered from the moment I witnessed it, and for the moment I had labeled it 'cultural intelligence.' I would labor to understand it in greater depth for the next several years.

That is—when I could find a moment to spare.

Idealism can intoxicate, but soon one is called back to mundane reality. I returned to Jamaica on fire, determined to save the world. I had come to the end of my student days. Soon I would be a graduate. An entire series of events soon dampened the flame. None of them extinguished the flame that had been lit at the Swiss conference.

Nonetheless, the height of that flame dimmed down somewhat as distractions and circumstances intervened. And I had come to a decision: the kind of life I wanted to lead led elsewhere—to America.

Emigrating to America was not an easy decision. I loved Jamaica. I still do.

But the truth was, as long back as the 1950's, members of my extended family (and Jamaican families are nothing if not extended) had one by one, family by family, begun emigrating to the United States. There was nothing surprising about that: back then Jamaica had been one of many emerging Third World nations. It was a joyous nation to belong to, but a nation where poverty was deep, struggle was hard, modernization was haphazard, and opportunities were limited.

America, as its Cold War propaganda repeatedly assured us, was very different: a land of wealth, freedom and opportunity. In the mid-Sixties, the Hart-Celler Act passed by America's Congress opened the door to the populations of emerging nations; and where one immigrant led, their families followed.

So, over the next few decades, members of my family and extended family emigrated to the United States.

On arriving in America, I asked myself, Was there a place for me in this New World? I asked advice and sent applications.

One day a letter arrived from an America institution of learning. Would I be interested in a teaching position?

The answer—yes!—went without saying. I was the son of a teacher. I loved the scholastic life. I was drunk with words, history, ideas, intellectual debate. Moreover, I believed in education: I knew how powerful and transformative it could be. I agreed with Socrates: the life of the mind was the only life worth living.

No sooner did I arrive than my excitement was tempered by realism. My student life had been an immersion in books and note-taking, thoughts and reflections. But I was an instructor now. I had strict schedules to follow. My days revolved around teaching and giving lectures. Those lectures covered world events, sociology, ancient and modern history, and the days flew by, filled with work.

Eventually I was called on to design entire programs and handle larger and larger administrative tasks. Teaching had become a full-time activity.

My idealism had by no means drained away. My experience at the Caux Conference left me determined to fulfill my life's goal: making some significant contribution to world peace; finding new tools to build genuine amity between discordant cultures. One day I realized that literally years had passed since the Conference. Yet I still felt that their goals were my goals. I was still passionate about making that my chief life purpose.

Social activism, charitable works, the intellectual life—none of these things have to die out entirely as we go about our everyday business. But they can. Our highest hopes and brightest aspirations can drown in a pool of entirely worthy and necessary distractions. I wanted more than a life of small satisfactions and moderate aspirations. It is said that the perfect is the enemy of the good, but a modest good can be the enemy of excellence also, and that can be tragic where the excellent is attainable.

I remember at the time reading an exceptionally powerful essay from *Upon Further Reflection* by B. F. Skinner called "Why We Are Not Acting To Save The World." Each of Skinner's explanations was profound, but one simple explanation really struck. We are simply too busy! Our individual lives draw us away from our collective lives, away from the common collective good. We turn away the big picture, forgetting that that comes at a price. In the end we all suffer. As Skinner would say, the immediate consequences of our behavior control us more strongly than the long-term consequences. That is, unless we can bring those long-term consequences into the immediate moment.

For better or for worse, I felt that I could make such a contribution in the area of peace studies and cultural analysis. I was determined to do so.

That did not necessarily mean putting aside a life of scholarship. Such a life would make it easier to develop my burgeoning thoughts and ideas about culture, it might even allow me to remain in touch with some of the many contacts I had made in Switzerland. In that regard my new sobriety was timely. I wanted to become a part of that international community of peacemakers. But when I considered them individually, who were they? Heads of State, leaders of industries, prominent journalists, notable authors—and scholars and educators.

These were people who had made their mark. They were people who had a great deal of substance to contribute. I realized that I would have to work, and work hard, to reach the level where I could make a comparable contribution in any field.

But if I worked and studied hard enough, could I make a scholarly contribution? Could I discover valuable lines of research? I was sure I could. I was already turning several over in my mind.

I was realistic about my hopes and my chances. It would take years, perhaps decades, to produce truly novel ideas, truly valuable scholarly work. It's one thing to be idealistic and inspired. It's quite another thing to make a notable contribution to the vast continent of academic knowledge. That takes serious and persistent effort. Serving the cause of world peace is not just a matter of spontaneously wanting to help others: it requires undertaking a serious and persistent course of self-development so as to be in a position to help others.

I could not make a scholarly contribution without undertaking further scholarly studies. That would take work—and time. I had already talked to a few of my teachers about continuing my education and becoming a Ph.D. Each encouraged me, but each also reminded me of the amount of work and thought needed even to write and defend a doctoral dissertation. It took some doctoral candidates half a lifetime.

But it was a step forward. A strong step, and a first

step. Eventually I would settle on a topic, a clarified and scaled-down subject to which my growing notes on cultural intelligence had called my attention. I realized the thoughts I'd crystallizing around the subject were vague, but there was a phenomenon—cultural competence—that was well established, not unrelated, and already a growing part of the literature.

Competence is not necessarily intelligence, just as a competently executed job is not necessarily a brilliant or groundbreaking one. But there was clearly a link. Could I find a way of expanding on that concept of competence, developing it with all the rigor demanded by academic scholarship, working out ways to apply it to newer and larger settings? I began making notes about that, too.

I had spent the past few years since the Caux Conference reading books, taking notes, building and rejecting theories and theses, thinking about the topic of my dissertation. I had been sowing seeds and tilling ground, reflecting but not really advancing that work. My time had not been wasted, but I realized that what I was doing was not enough. If I wanted to make the strongest contribution possible, I would need to educate myself to the strongest extent possible.

Now that I was living in America, such possibilities began to open before me. And before me too was one of the most extraordinary multicultural environments in all human history—in itself a subject of study without parallel.

Chapter Four

Impressions
of
America

Impressions
of
America

Once arrived in America, I focused on pursuing my postgraduate education.

With a population of over 330 million people and a continental land mass, the United States has the highest number of universities in the world, with over six thousand higher educational institutions. Those searching for the ideal college, be it large or small, urban or rural, are sure to find it.

And when it comes to program availability, the United States is the land of opportunity too. Undergraduate and postgraduate degrees span nearly every discipline. There's a program for every interest and ambition in America—from the classic and conventional, to the absurd and the esoteric.

America fascinated me. Fascinated me as a student of culture.

Seriously, what student of culture is not simply bewitched by America as a cultural entity? What nation spends more on peace, or has been so devastating in its wars? What nation is more open to diversity, or has been more scarred by slavery and racism? What nation is more verbally committed to equality, or more staggeringly marred by the grossest economic inequality? What nation has done more to promote itself as the model of an advanced First World society, or been more vilified and excoriated as the last dying fortress of Late Capitalism? America is modernity, and its culture and technology and mores are modernity's Siren Song, a vortex into which all other contemporary cultures are drawn.

America also provides so many puzzles and insights into cultural coexistence that no student of culture can ignore it. It is one of the few societies in human history that explicitly put itself forward as universal— that has continually preened itself as a paradigm that every nation should adopt, and one day will adopt. Democracy, Equality, the Separation of Church and State. Freedom of Speech, Competition and Opportunity. Capitalism, Civil Rights. Of late, Equity and Social Justice. From its inception America has presented itself to the world as a grand and ultimate experiment in human freedom and self-governance, and commentators from Alexis de Tocqueville to an army of present-day pundits have poked, praised, probed, and groaned over the carnage and triumphs of its fluctuations. Moreover, it has not contented itself to be a model. Like its great adversary, the Soviet Union, it has asserted that all races, creeds, ethnicities could be and would inevitably be subsumed in its egalitarian embrace. Imperialist liberation, in one and the same contradictory expansion.

Was this country indeed what it claimed to be—the pattern of the future, the path that every nation must take in its trek into the world of today and tomorrow?

Or is that even a prediction anymore? What nation is not Americanized to some extent by now? What nation is not permeated by American pop music, by its Marvel Comics films, its Culture Wars, its video games, its blue jeans and billionaires, its superheroes, and its Big Macs? What nation has better mastered, if unconsciously, a cultural imperialism that has occupied not merely the territory of other nations but their mind?

That more than anything made America a nation that I needed to spend years studying. Since my childhood, America had been presented to me as the last superstate, the first rough version of the globalist future of a unified humanity. It was the fabled nation of immigrants, synthesized out of all nations, all peoples, all races, all religions. Supposedly its doors were open to everyone, and out of that multiplicity of cultures had emerged not only a stable, functioning, viable society, but the richest and most powerful society in human history. A continent-spanning society in which, for all its loud self-criticism and frequent turmoil, vastly disparate people and cultures lived in—relative—peace.

The USSR had reached for a similar vision: it had forged a superstate harboring over a hundred nationalities, over twice that number of languages, numerous races, and ethnicities. But that superstate had been held together unnaturally, by brute force from above and through ideological totalitarianism. When blind faith in the ideology faded, and when the brute force relaxed, it collapsed. It was a failed experiment.

America had forged itself out of a not dissimilar brutality—the forced labor of African slaves, the near-genocide of its indigenous Native American population, ultimately out of a Civil War that left nearly three-quarters of a million of its people dead. It had indeed founded itself on explicit principles of white supremacy and gender supremacy. America too had its dark side.

But it was not reducible to that dark side. It had learned to evolve. Struggle by struggle, amendment by amendment, it time and again showed itself capable of expanding its notions of freedom and human rights to more and more of its people. That expansion was still not complete, yet it did not rest: it strove for ever greater completeness, and that too was a fascinating cultural process to watch. To watch and to learn from.

Here was a European colony that had not only thrown off its colonial rule, but come to surpass all Europe in power and wealth. A nation of slaveholders overthrown by Abolitionists. A nation whose entry into World War Two spelled the end of racist National Socialism. There was the Bill of Rights. The founding of the United Nations. The Civil Rights Act. The Immigration Act.

Imperfect as its beginnings might have been, tawdry as its present-day actions sometimes were, American history displayed a burning, continual push to transcend its own flaws and limitations. It seemed to me that this was an extraordinarily idealistic nation; and since I was and still am unashamedly idealistic myself, its moral aspiration moved me. It ever strove to better itself. I tried to study it dispassionately, but that took great discipline, for I knew that I too wanted to be a part of that striving.

I nonetheless sought to temper that favorable inclination with cooler analysis. America was more than a set of idealistic sentiments: it was a collection of actual cultural institutions and a set of real-life cultural processes. How it presented itself, and what it thought of itself and what others thought of it, were rhetorical layers which every good student would note but would also need to peel away if he or she wanted to understand the mechanisms underneath.

I wanted to understand those mechanisms, because I wanted the peoples of the world to live in prosperity and peace. Was the American model the best way to that goal? Was it, practically speaking, the best way that history had come up with so far? Such a case could be made. A case could also be made that in the wake of the Soviet collapse, the American model was the only one left standing, so that model would inevitably spread. The European Union was said to have formed itself by taking the United States as its model. Perhaps other collections of nations would as well. Or perhaps they would simply and willingly be absorbed into it. One day, so some said, every nation would join America as a new State, and the entire world would be America.

Was that true? Was it even possible? Or was America what critics claimed, the consummate imperialist ogre of our time, oppressing people of color, debasing the working class with bread and circuses, incinerating Japanese in nuclear flames and Arabs in saturation bombing as it trampled nations underfoot in its march toward world hegemony?

I suspected the truth was something more moderate than the over-ripe rhetoric of both its friends and its foes. But I needed to see it function to know. And I needed to know if I was to advance in my understanding of culture and cultural intelligence.

My many years of living here have led me to mixed conclusions. Personally, they've been fruitful years. I was certainly not wrong in thinking that America would provide me with significant cultural insights. Nor was I wrong in thinking I would thrive professionally. I quickly found a teaching position, and soon after that branched out to serve a few NGOs. I finished my dissertation here; I was granted my Doctorate here. Eventually I would find a spot at the United Nations and serve at UNESCO. For me, at least, the great American promise, the promise of opportunity, has proved true.

I am grateful to America for this, and for much else. America has done and continues to do a tremendous amount of good for the world. As I've said, America was a founder of the League of Nations, a pillar of the United Nations, the place a tremendous number of NGOs and global charities and organization called home. It's the source of funding for any number of good causes and worthwhile peace initiatives. There are a multitude of good, smart, compassionate people here deeply committed to the ideal of a better world for everyone.

But—for me as a student of cultures—the cultural reality of America remains ambiguous. One should never underestimate the capacity of this great nation to overcome itself, and leap, sometimes heroically, sometimes violently, to a new and higher level. Still, the reality of America is not the same thing as its promise, and its great light is sometimes balanced by an equivalent darkness.

My time in Jamaica between the Caux Conference and my arrival in the United States were focused more on my personal life and career rather than on larger world events and what they could tell us about peace and cultural cooperation. But there was one major world event that no one could ignore. The event we remember as 9/11, the Iraq War; or, as the American media put it, of the "War On Terror."

It was not an auspicious time. When suicide bombers struck the Twin Towers on September 11, more than the Towers fell. Whole networks of globe-spanning peace initiatives vanished along with them. Watching the war unfold was like attending entire seminars, not in cultural intelligence, but in cultural insanity.

Any reasonable outsider could see that a horrible crime had been committed against innocent civilians. The perpetrators themselves were dead, but clearly it was right and proper to bring those orchestrating that crime to justice. One could imagine the ringleaders being turned over by their respective governments to the World Court, and appropriate judgment being rendered.

But that is not what the world outside America saw on its television screens. What they saw were American news programs announcing that terrorist war had been declared upon the whole of America by an 'Axis of Evil' compromising several malevolent nations and a good part of a global religion, Islam. These actors were criminals, America had been injured, America was threatened, and America was going to prevent all those it deemed responsible from ever being a threat again— by wiping them out of existence.

The reaction of many of my friends and colleagues in the Third World (and especially in the Middle East) was dread. They feared that a maddened and infuriated America was going to use the incident to select victim nations at random in the Third World and obliterate them. It was not a matter of justice or rationality. It was a matter of outrage, fury, unbridled and thoughtless revenge. A tantrum was about to be thrown by the greatest technological superpower in human history. Blood was about to flow, and flow in torrents. America was becoming, in the terrible phrase of George Orwell, "a boot stamping on a human face—forever."

It did not stamp forever. But stamp it did. The American descent into international vengeance was horrible to behold—horrible, yet (though it pains me to say it) from the viewpoint of cultural intelligence, fascinating. America seemed not only to be making the least intelligent moves—to many outside the United States, it seemed to be literally going mad.

The attack had been done by Saudi nationals. Yet America ignored the Saudis, and went on to decimate and occupy Iraq, and to hurl itself against Afghanistan for the next nineteen years—only to leave both in failure.

America justified the destruction of Iraq by claims of evidence that the Iraqis had 'weapons of mass destruction.' There was no such evidence. Iraq's leader was nonetheless hung by the neck and images of his corpse were broadcast across the world, images that cemented America's image as a self-appointed global executioner. Soon images of torture from Abu Ghraib blackened world respect for America even further.

The 9/11 attackers said the bombing was in retaliation for American interference in the Muslim world. America went on to interfere further, enough to eradicate between a hundred thousand and a million Muslim lives.

These assaults cost America over six trillion dollars,

sent the strongest economy on Earth into a crashing tailspin, and resulted in the President and Party authorizing it being voted out of office.

From being the world's leading and indeed only superpower, a model for the world, America sank into internal division, a growing hyperpolarization that continues to widen even today, and brought upon itself tremendous foreign detestation, a global contempt that still persists. From the peak of being the world's sole superpower after the end of Communism, it has sunk to a nation that is now supposedly being surpassed by Communist China, and one whose leading newspapers repeatedly feature brooding articles about popular insurrection and even Civil War.

What could possibly account for this complete collapse of cultural intelligence? It simply made no sense whatever as a matter of rational statecraft.

Yet upon reflection, I realized it made a tremendous amount of sense — once I began to frame it in emotional terms. No, it was not a case of rational statecraft. America had been traumatized. It was lashing out, striking back. The speeches of its leaders, the material presented by its news commentators, were exactly the sort of outraged bravura and livid dehumanization one could expect from someone deeply injured. Its actions made no sense in rational terms. But they made a great deal of sense in psychological terms.

Even the terrorists' actions made sense in those terms. Would the tremendous industrial and military power of America be set back even one iota by the death of a few thousand civilians in two skyscrapers? America lost more than that number of lives in traffic accidents every month.

Would not such an attack more likely supercharge and accelerate and violently increase American militarism and aggression? Assaulting America in the way they did was a venture in which both sides could only lose—and lose tremendously. Which is exactly what happened, and which was only what could happen.

Why then did it happen? Like others, I rummaged around for rational explanations; but soon I realized that I was witnessing cultural relations, failed cultural relations driven by emotion, not reason. The only question was why the institutions and leadership and cultural safeguards that should have tempered that reaction were frail enough that they could be so swiftly and instantly torn away.

That single question, however, was not the only one. What accounted for the stark discrepancies in media coverage? Watching conservative American reporting by Fox and foreign reporting by Al Jazeera was to pass through two separate parallel worlds. America had a supposedly free press. Surely one could expect a thousand opinions. Instead, the response was unanimous support for the President's policies—at first. As soon as the policies were seen to be so palpably failing, there came equally unanimous condemnation.

Yet the policies continued throughout the Bush years, even through the Obama administration, flowering in the infamous ban of immigration from Muslim nations by Donald Trump. The War on Terror was never won, and under the latest administration, only the focus has changed: now the official spotlight has been placed on domestic terrorists—the American people themselves.

As an American citizen, I have followed this process with grief. But it also gave me, as it must give any student of culture and cultural harmony, much on which to reflect. Once a tiny colony, America has grown into the strongest and wealthiest nation in the world. The opportunities it offers its citizens seem boundless. Its success spoke of intelligence, and yet its reaction to the attack on 9/11 was terrifying in its mindlessness. It's not too much to say that that incident, or rather America's response, marked the beginning of a decline that has proceeded from that day to this.

Yet seeing that decline, attempting to trace its causes, began to change my position on the nature and interaction of cultures, and, I believe, deepen it.

I began to give much more weight to the psychological aspect of cultures.

Of course, to see cultures as almost sentient hive-minds, as Spenglerian individuals that grow and flourish into distinct eccentric personalities, then descend into senility, is, needless to say, pure romanticism. We cannot replace data by anthropomorphizing, or with intuition.

Yet it is not too much—or so I came to believe—to perceive something of a psychological outline to different cultures, and to be able to ground that through an assessment of objective data. The workaholism of Japanese culture, the manifest sense of superiority of Confederate slaveholders, the cultural cohesion of Judaism from its beginnings to today, manifest themselves in behavior, and behaviors amenable to objective study which have predictive scope.

I found myself wondering. If there are psychological dimensions to cultural behavior, and so to cultural interaction, might there be psychological solutions as well? I began to explore the literature, and (as always) took more notes.

I also—perhaps through sheer weariness at the chronic sour despair of news headlines—began at that time reading into the literature of utopia. Buddhism, surprisingly, offered some poignant images of social peace. I had regarded Buddhism as a very individualistic path of personal meditation that at its heart counseled turning one's back on the world, but now I found myself delving intermittently into Pure Land Buddhism, into Chogyam Trungpa and material about the coming perfect Buddhist community of Shambhala, where present-day egoistic conflict would be put aside. I didn't feel that Buddhist social activism was the answer to America's current problems, but those efforts, with their appeals not only to active social engagement, but to inner engagement, struck an enduring chord.

I was very taken as well—positively and negatively— with the social reflections of B. F. Skinner. Skinner was, after all, at one time was considered to be one of, if not the, leading American psychologists. Who would know Americans better? Moreover, his novel Walden Two seemed a detailed blueprint of exactly the sort of evolving Utopia I was seeking: a society of peace and stability marked by a constant application of cultural intelligence: intelligence actively applied to a given culture with the goal of shaping it into a stable peaceful community gratifying to all its members. Skinner too was an idealist, but more to the point, he was a profoundly data-driven idealist whose utopian projections were anything but fantasies, rooted as they were in decades of the most precise behavioral study.

I was especially taken by his insistence that the most effective and desirable societies need be non-punitive in nature. For Skinner, humans and human behavior were driven by positive reinforcement. (Which is not exactly the same thing as 'rewards,' though that understanding is close enough for my purpose here.) The result of an interaction must be positive in nature for the participant for that action to continue. It need not be ecstatic, or overwhelmingly positive. But if it is even mildly positive it will tend to be repeated.

If the result of an action is negative, however, one of three things result: flight, counterattack, or passivity. Strike someone, and they will either run away, strike you back, or simply stand there and take your blows till you tire. But none of those things will bind you together or give you the willing allegiance or friendship or enduring support that you want. Sooner or later the punished individual goes away—assuming he or she does not respond with a violence that destroys you.

This simple formula, confirmed through thousands of experiments on everything from mice to graduate students, explained so much. Enslave a people: either they run away, engage in slave revolts, or simply suffer till they can run away or revolt. Oppress a nation: some emigrate (flight), others become terrorists (counterattack). Why had America lasted so long while the Soviet Union fell? Because America promised that if you worked hard and lived lawfully, you would be rewarded with prosperity. The Soviet Union demanded that you work hard and live lawfully or face the Gulag. One proffered a carrot. The other a stick.

An over-simplification? Yes. But one containing a kernel of truth. Bin Laden could not have been clearer about his motives. He felt that Muslims and Arabs were being made to suffer by tyrannical elites in Islamic states, and by Israeli expansionism. Who funded and supported those elites and Israel? America. The people with whom he had identified had been struck, and he was striking back.

This is not to blame American policy in the Middle East for 9/11—though many have made exactly that claim. Rather it is to point out that Skinner made an extremely well-grounded psychological case for basing societies, and basing social action, on positive and not on punitive grounds. His vision of a human future completely dispensing with the need for coercion startled me, but also resonated with me strongly.

Alas, his vision came with too many demerits to completely enlist me.

Skinner had the unfortunate tendency to present his quite valid social and behavioral insights in a package that included his philosophy, and his philosophy was unacceptable. He was a thorough-going materialist and atheist who denied that human freedom had any reality at all. Behavior was shaped by consequences and a behaviorist elite would—positively!—fine-tune the thoughts and actions of everyone in behaviorist society. You would be manipulated into feeling free, even as you were entirely stripped of all freedom. It was not a product I wanted to buy.

In addition, his behavioral Utopia, Walden Two, had the further demerit of being intrinsically small. Skinner made an interesting comment in that regard which stayed with me for some years, eventually shaping some of my future thoughts. He said that behavior was strongest when communities were small and personal. In a community of 200 to 250 people, he said, everyone in the community knew everyone personally, face-to-face, and interacted with them regularly. Under such conditions, cruelty or mistreatment would find it hard to flourish, since there would be an immediate, negative, felt response.

A fighter pilot could drop bombs and incinerate entire populations with comparative indifference. After all, they were people he did not know, suffering from effects which he did not see. But carnage on such scope was impossible face-to-face, person-to-person.

It was a point I would remember, but it seemed to have little value for someone interested in global peace between existing nations. For Skinner's principles to operate, the world would have to dissolve into thousands of millions of tiny villages. They might be peaceful and even happy, but it was too far from the world of today to seriously consider.

In the course of all this teaching, thinking and study, I also found the time for some utopian consolations, and insights, in something quite far from academia—one of the iconic perennials of American pop culture: Star Trek. As cultural studies go, I must ask the reader's indulgence! I realize that Kirk and Spock have not contributed much worth thinking about to the scholarly literature on peace studies.

Yet I found myself watching the program, in particular Next Generation and Voyager, as surprisingly revelatory images of American multiculturalism, or at least of America's hopes for multiculturalism. For Star Trek's Federation is nothing if not America writ large. Not only has global humanity been brought together into one unity, following the American ideal of endless expansion and continual scientific and technological progress, collaboration with alien races and cultures is entirely commonplace. Human, Vulcan, Klingon, Android and green tentacled multi-pedal blob all worked and socialized together in sublime harmony.

There is only one catch: the cultural differences are all subsumed if not erased under the Federation ethos. Even the casual viewer could see that however alien their features or origins, every Star Trek character would be as perfectly comfortable staffing an American advertising agency as a starship.

Permeating the *surface* multiculturalism is a bland underlying monoculture. For all their differences, Star Trek's aliens are all Americans. Rather appealing Americans, to be sure, and going about their jobs quite efficiently! Yet among the humans as among the aliens, serious religious faith is absent, as is ideology. We never see democratic processes or economic struggle or class disparity. Other planets may still be roiled by these things, but the Federation has passed beyond them—into what exactly, we are never really told.

The series remains well worth watching. Its creator, Gene Roddenberry, said when proposing it that he wanted to create a future world in which racism, poverty, hatred, division— "all that stuff"—was just gone, vanished into the darkness of pre-history, and good riddance. I still find it refreshing to break into the sunlight of such a world view now and then, and I think seeing its image on the deck of the Enterprise has done many people some genuine good.

At the same time, I wish there had been a few images of how humanity managed to get from point A to B, and of how that sunlit world manages to govern and sustain itself. Ah well, perhaps in some new future series. Let us be content with what we have, and continue to believe that reaching such a world is possible.

I don't want to give the impression that understanding America's reaction to 9/11 took up most of my mental space. I had a great deal else to focus on—"making life" in America, in a strange yet familiar land. And it was familiar, eerily familiar, for which of us has not grown up watching American TV, listening to American rock music, tasting American fast food?

To dwell only on the surface of America is to be distracted, however. It is often said that America is a "proposition nation," a polity built on a set of ideas, principally the idea that "all men are created equal," and deserve equal treatment before the law, and equal opportunity. It was one of the few societies in human history that explicitly put itself forward as universal— that announced itself as a closely woven pattern of social interaction that everyone would and should one day emulate. America, the grand and ultimate experiment in human freedom and self- governance! An experiment whose impressive mixed results to date remain somewhat controversial.

Did I find this country to be what it claimed to be— the presence of the future, the path that every nation must take in its journey into the modern world? Did it live up to its ideal? No. But then what country ever has? Few countries even have an ideal. They are simply what they are, cast up on the shores of the modern world by history, doing their best to get by.

America, by contrast, seems always eagerly craving to transform itself into some perfect version of itself, and either inflating its aspirations as being far more realized than they are (the preferred position of pundits on the American right) or exaggerating its imperfections into perfect vileness (often the position of pundits on the American left). Both are a form of idealism I reject: idealism without realism.

To someone not born in America, the nation displays itself as a series of paradoxes. "Dedicated to the proposition that all men are created equal," it had been a slave society from its very beginnings. Home to hundreds of cultures and languages and tens of millions of immigrants, it is assailed for being incorrigibly conformist and racist. It is the Great Melting Pot in which none of the ingredients ever completely melt.

But mythologies and PR aside, what was it actually like? What could I learn about it through direct cultural interaction?

As it turned out, I learned a great deal about peace and culture from America—but not very much that heartened me. America proved to be neither the Utopia its friends claim nor the moral and social disaster its enemies assert. It's a kind of society I had never encountered and probably would not have thought possible till I came to live permanently. Yet it exists, and in many respects even thrives.

My problem with America was this. In other

multicultural countries, the subcultures are tolerated or abrasive, dominant or subordinate, joined in mutual respect or locked in combat. In America, people of very different cultures seem to function together well enough in the workplace, but outside the workplace they rarely connect. I found that Americans have really very little social cohesion, very few close relationships, not even in the dominant culture—perhaps especially so in the dominant culture. It all works: America is a functional, a prosperous, in many ways a highly successful society.

But somehow it manages to be a society without being a community. I could not quite understand that. At first.

Of course, teaching at universities, working in the area of administration, training fellow educators, and tutoring students—occasionally difficult students—introduce you to all sorts. I met Americans rich and poor, influential and obscure, upper class and underclass. I found myself easily generalizing; for which I must apologize, since I know very well, Reader, that there are always exceptions to every rule, and America is very rich in exceptions. In generalizing, therefore, I ask your indulgence. But there are a few things about American culture that struck me with considerable force.

First: a tremendous distinction must be made between immigrants, especially new immigrants, and Americans who have been born here and have lived and drifted (I do not use the word lightly) through America for generations. When an immigrant arrives, he brings with him his culture. The first day I arrived here from Jamaica, I was a Jamaican, and the first day an Afghan refugee arrives here he is an Afghan. One can learn the language, master the cultural norms, be granted citizenship, sincerely abide by its laws, and honor its unwritten social rules; yet one's original cultural residue will remain.

The following generation—the children of that immigrant—are like mermaids. They are half fish and half human. They have an American personality that they don when going outside, almost like a mask. They speak English when outside, they groan over the football and basketball contests, they eat junk food along with everyone else in the cafeteria; but when they come home, they speak their parents' language, they eat their parents' ethnic dishes, they discuss what is happening in the 'Old Country.' They are fluent in both cultures, though they may lean towards one or the other. Eventually they are enveloped more and more in their "American side," though a very few may come to reject that American side with literal violence.

In the generation following, all trace of their grandparents' culture is wiped out. The grandchildren are as American as any other American, and if they are visibly Indian or Japanese or whatnot, they resent being pegged as someone 'exotic.'

Rightly so. For one of the most striking things about America is how amazingly culturally homogenous they are. In Europe, in Africa, if you travel a hundred miles, everything changes—the language, the laws, the food, the fashions, the news reports, the currency, the whole environment. In America, you can get on a plane at one end of the country, fly 3,000 miles, and when you get off the plane? You see the same MacDonalds, the same

Burger King, the same New York Times on the same rack in the same place in the similarly designed grocery megastore selling the same sorts of brand name food, as the same pop tunes from the 50's and 70's croon out of the speakers.

Yes, there are some regional distinctions. But I am still surprised at how minimal they are. Americans still seem to me all to drown in the same coffee, gobble the same pizza, watch the same football matches, and spend hours in front of the same shows on the television set. Older viewers watch television dramas—soup operas, cop shows, and the news, which is ideologically divided. Younger viewers play violent video games.

Yet despite the near-universal similarities, there are very few gatherings. People work, drive home, enter their apartments or suburban cocoons, and—unless they go out to eat— remain there.

There are certainly people in every culture who have close family ties and close friendships. But Americans are a curiously atomized people. They rarely appeared bound to their neighborhoods or towns or villages. The feeling seems to be that adulthood requires them to go hundreds or thousands of miles away to college, and after that, to travel wherever work is available. They drift, like tumbleweeds in the America West, and rarely stay for very long where they stop. When the wind blows again, they move on, rarely returning to their previous locations.

Family life too is disconnected. Economic pressure mandates both parents work, and so children are raised in Day Care till being sent to school. Divorce rates are extremely high, and rising. Most marriages fail, and so most children find themselves experiencing visitations from multiple parents.

In terms of race, despite an enormous Hispanic population (the second highest in the nation) and ever-increasing immigration from Asian nations and the Middle East, nearly everything is seen from a paradigm of black and white. Or rather, black versus white.

There, relations are very poor. Black Americans and white Americans have very different cultures, especially Americans who live in the inner cities as opposed to whites in the suburbs or rural areas. Both these areas are tremendously segregated. Not by bayonets, but by cost: suburban homes may easily approach half a million or more in cost (funded, like education, by massive debt); inner city homes, owned by landlords, not tenants, cost tens of thousands. Yet the houses in suburbia are mere collections of houses, not communities. One can drive through for miles and never see a human face.

Curiously, I've observed that among black Americans there is a great deal of political solidarity, but little personal solidarity. Black Americans will vote for the Democratic Party at rates of over 94%. Yet black-on-black crime in black neighborhoods is among the highest in the nation. The situation is reversed for white Americans. Crime in the overwhelmingly white suburbs is minimal, but political animosity is passionate, nearly livid. Liberal white Americans, the more educated and financially well-off of the two, vote Democrat in numbers rivaling that of black Americans, while Conservative white Americans, who generally less well-educated, less fiscally well-off, and lower in social status, vote overwhelmingly Republican. Both (from what one sees of their respective news programming) seem utterly to despise one another, although with an interesting distinction: conservatives appear to find Americans to be merely fools, whereas liberals appear to find conservatives contemptible villains. To the conservative, the liberal is intellectually wrong. To the liberal, the conservative is morally suspect.

I soon came to feel that relations between white Americans seemed to perfectly mirror Marx's picture of class conflict, the liberal upper class at odds with the conservative lower class. Why the white lower class—largely the working class—would lean conservative rather than liberal (essentially the party of democratic socialism, which traditionally is the party of the working class) continues to puzzle me. Why the white upper class—the wealthier group, which owns, invests, and is institutionally connected—favors the redistributionist party is yet another puzzle. I haven't resolved it; I merely note it, and note that black Americans, in my experience, seem mercifully free of this acid mutual detestation.

Aside from this strange inorganic quality to American life, the greatest shock I experienced was America's startling ignorance of history and geography. I would tutor students in Washington D.C. who seemed to think that Joan of Arc was the mother of Noah, or that Lenin was one of the Beatles. China was what rich people used for dishes. The rest of the world seemed not to exist. Nor did most of America: there was New York City, there was Los Angeles, and between them stretched "flyover country," a vast desert populated with toothless extras from *Deliverance*. The rest of the world was where you went on a two-day vacation.

Mind you, this is no reflection whatever on American

scholarship. My American colleagues were as competent and well-read as anyone in the world. Nor is this a reflection on the nation's general intelligence. The average American seemed bright enough. But even otherwise bright-seeming Americans would startle me by how ill-informed or even completely uninformed they sometimes were. I would say that I was from Jamaica. Was that in Puerto Rico? Was it a country, or a city?

I finally put my finger on what, culturally, bothered me about America.

It made me think of Hegel's phrase, "bad infinity." Hegel defines "bad infinity" as a kind of infinity in which the aspiration to overcome the finite never succeeds but always remains the same. America too had this same sort of infinite ambition combined with an intangible vacancy, an empty stasis.

Perhaps a more prosaic way of putting it is that in America people of different cultures worked together well enough but did not like each other very much. What brought them together was the need to make money. After the day was done, each drove off to separate lives, closed the door, and turned on the television. And that was all.

It had been my feeling that, if world peace were ever to truly come, it would be because people would learn to transcend their tribal animosity and learn to embrace and cherish other cultures while still revering their own.

America presented me with an entire continent of people seemingly indifferent not only to other cultures but indifferent even to their own. Compared to the joy and yet rudeness of Jamaica, the oppression and yet idealism of Cuba, the color and rebellion and passions of so many other nations in the world, America seemed shallow, flat, colorless and loveless.

And yet it worked! I had a sudden vision of a world society of peace, but without love; of tolerance, but without respect, even without self-respect; an atomized society of isolated individuals living half-lives, held together only by the profit motive. Yet it was a world of peace and tolerance. A world lacking only some existential spark—the humanity that would make it worth living.

Before coming to America, I had felt that the problem of cultural compatibility was in some ways very simple. Cultures were compatible or they weren't! If they were, or if they could learn to be compatible, they would live together in relative peace, ideally in a symbiotic relationship where both parties benefitted. If they weren't compatible, the result would be separation, nonviolent if possible, or rebellious segregation if not.

Not till I came to America did I imagine that a multicultural society could simply lack all interest in other cultures and even in its own culture, and yet still be viable, even successful—that it could be coherent and incoherent, united and separate, at the same time. In ways the coronavirus pandemic only exacerbated this strange American quality of being alone together: a nation held together not by personal familiarity and affection, but by Zoom.

I suppose that in some ways, this is the American genius: the famous 'separation of powers' in which sovereignty is divided. The Framers apparently gambled that social unity would not be needed in a world where advancing one's own economic interests required a bare minimum of marginally polite cooperation with those of others. Such a bare minimum would emerge naturally if both economic actors wished to survive. It was a model not of a community but a marketplace. That was not very much to tie the traders in this marketplace together, but then America was nothing if not an experiment: perhaps not much would be enough.

Perhaps. But I felt that that minimum was too bare, too minimal, and at the heart of a great deal of palpable American unhappiness.

I came to see the American Way of Life as an unfulfilled promise. Not that there was anything terribly unpleasant about it. Americans were pleasant enough. Some, indeed, were exceptionally kind, friendly, charming, even brilliant. But on the whole, what peace and stability I could see around me, while admirable in many ways, seemed empty, a strange intersection of Disneyland and the void.

It was too easy to be satisfied with this lesser version of peace and tolerance. This was not a vivid world rich with the appreciation of other cultures and one's own. It was a wan and bloodless version of that vision.

Even now I cannot quite square the dynamism of American history with the almost anemic quality of what I see today of its tenuous social bonds.

But the freedom and economic rewards of that society still appear to attract people, and to bind them here all their lives. Perhaps that *is* enough, after all.

Hobbes had once described society as a "War of All against All." His vision was dark, and America refuted it. It proved that a society could indeed exist by means of mutual service and cooperation, provided such service and cooperation was profitable enough for each individual involved.

But can such a society be said to truly thrive? Was America a culture, or simply a vast yawning workspace where different and indifferent people collect to perform a well-paid function?

Reading its passionate history, its vertiginous achievements, its idealistic origins, I felt that it had once been far more than this, and I hoped and believed it could one day be so again.

Chapter Five

Writing
A
Dissertation

Writing A Dissertation

When I wrote earlier that I spent my first few years in America teaching and adjusting to American life, I perhaps should have said, 'adjusting and re-adjusting.' For America is a chameleon: its colors change with each new Presidency.

Of note were the George W. Bush years, as U.S. involvement in Iraq was crashing and taking the American economy with it. The Obama presidency was like another country: everything brightened. Its motto was "Hope and Change," and there was indeed a fresh sense of hope and change in the air. Yet the war dragged on regardless, the economy remained torpid, and polarization in politics and in the culture only worsened. The surprise election of Trump turned hope into dread and change into reaction. An entire range of American norms were thrown off a cliff, and political polarization became incandescent. The pinwheel revolved once again in 2020: on the first day of the Biden Administration, the new President reversed every Trump Executive Order.

I note these changes neither with praise nor blame.

I simply want to record what new arrivals to America encounter: a topsy-turvy shifting landscape that never appears to stop shifting. One gets dizzy. Especially if one is working to better understand other cultures, and has American culture beneath one's magnifying glass. The object of study changes every time one returns to it!

Real life was my anchor. Luckily, I had more mundane and demanding things needing my attention. Where should I live, for whom or what should I work?

The answer to the second question was easy: I followed the direction set by my educational background and experience and continued to teach and lecture. The answer to the first was easy too: In addition to my family being there, I chose to live in Washington D.C., for that was where hundreds if not thousands of non-governmental organizations and efforts were headquartered.

Why did that matter so much? Because the inspiration I had experienced at the Caux conference had not only inspired me, but also left me with a practical insight: the peacemakers of this world are a network. That network may be loose and uncoordinated, it may contain smaller and more idiosyncratic sub-networks, it may be fragmented and scattered. But by and large those who actively and effectively strive for peace often know of one another, and not infrequently come together and work together.

I wanted to enter that network. So, in addition to my teaching, I sought to find a charitable non-profit or non-governmental organization to which I could contribute.

What could I contribute? Here my educational skills and my cultural focus came together.

Teaching students in Washington D.C. is a daily

encounter with cultural diversity. Sometimes it's an encounter (I nearly wrote 'collision') with subcultural diversity: I found that black American inner-city students, students from Hispanic neighborhoods, Asian neighborhoods, white urban students, had strikingly little in common culturally. University-level students have an equally striking high number of students from nations other than America.

There are educators who virtually lecture to their classes, almost indifferently, as though to one undifferentiated mass. However, I wanted my students not only to learn, but to learn tolerance and mutual forbearance—even mutual appreciation. American conformity had been a matter of sociological cliche in the 1950's, but since then it had come to waken to an almost new conception of itself: a new sense of America as not only multicultural but as striving for a more multicultural ideal.

The rhetoric was noble, but the practice, like so much in America, was improvisatory and chaotic. Like so many Americans nowadays, my students seemed to have found themselves thrown into not a single American culture but into an explicitly multicultural society, yet without a guidebook on how to maneuver within that surging multiplicity gracefully. I made it part of my teaching 'style' to model tolerance and cross-cultural maneuverability, and—gently—to foster that maneuverability among my students. To help my students develop greater cultural competence.

I did not think of it at the time as 'Cultural Competence,' a full-blown official skill set in capital letters with an academic sheen and a tightly defined skill set and training flowchart all its own. I was simply an educator from one culture, Jamaica, a peaceful and stable multicultural nation, encountering American students (and, later, Americans in organizations) whose own racial and religious and scholastic and corporate subcultures often seemed to jar and clash. Not badly enough for the system as a whole to fall apart, true, but enough to produce that strange social incoherence, that integrated set of segregations, that dysfunctional functionality, that marked American social life.

I called on my own personal experience to help students bridge that gap, but naturally I soon turned to books and studies to supplement my efforts. I learned that Cultural Competence in capital letters was indeed a tightly-defined area of research, training and implementation. I began reading all that I could about the subject and applying it—informally but successfully—in academic and professional contexts.

In time I began thinking about adding to the scholarly literature on the subject via the writing of my dissertation. Cultural competence was certainly a subject of interest to me, and of value to others. It was also something with which I was intimately familiar, both as a Jamaican, an immigrant, and a teacher of multicultural students, an educator and administrator engaging with multicultural colleagues.

But the prospect of professional activism pulled me away. Soon after settling myself in the local Washington D.C. academic community, I received an offer from a non-profit working to help people in distressed areas. Here was my chance to do good! I accepted the position, without discontinuing my teaching, or putting my dissertation studies on hold; and so shouldered forward under a rather crushing workload.

I don't wish to go into too much detail about my service with non-profits, for I found it both very positive in some ways and very disappointing in others. But I don't want to be seen as lavishing praise or heaping blame upon any specific organization, because, having since become familiar with a number of such organizations, many seem to be in much the same situation; I think my comments apply generally. In one respect, that situation is glorious: non-profits do in fact help others across the globe: they do indeed feed the hungry, clothe the naked, shelter the homeless. If there is anywhere in this world where an intersection of Christianity and capitalism exists, it is in these non-profit entities. They are embodiments of charity in their intentions and their results, and I hail them all.

Their actual operations, however, are more often focused, of necessity, on organizational and economic survival rather than charity. Since they do not, after all, make a profit, some other entity that does has to support them. I was rather disheartened to see how much non-profit effort is given over to incessant fund-raising efforts and finding donors. Governments, grant-dispensing organizations, philanthropic institutions, individual donors of wealth, grassroots organizations—the bulk of non-profit work involves constantly canvassing all of these and more for donations. That work is critically necessary. Without that work, little if any charitable action can be undertaken.

That said, one wants to help the needy, not spend the bulk of one's time and efforts soliciting funds. Over time the urgent need for funds becomes, if not exactly spiritually corrosive, spiritually disheartening. At times I felt as though the entire day was spent soliciting funds purely so that the organization could afford to solicit funds again the next day.

I also soon learned that nearly every non-profit corporate entity is, unavoidably, a corporate entity—it has an internal hierarchy, significant legal restrictions, iron-clad financial limitations, and a truly onerous burden of office politics and internal bickering. It might be inspired by its vision and motivated by humanitarian *caritas*, but in terms of day-to-day operations, papers needed to be shuffled, office expenditures accounted for, performance reviews done, and hierarchy obeyed. I am not being critical when I say this. These things are organizationally inevitable and obligatory. They allow charitable undertakings to be made.

But this is the bureaucracy of charity, not charity itself. Such activities may support charitable activities— though often enough they retard it—but are not in themselves charitable. As with fund-raising, I found much of my time spent in activities that often seemed beside the point. As a teacher, I spent most of my time teaching. I could see the fruits of my efforts in my students' growing understanding, and I could see that it was good. As a non-profit do-gooder, I did not always feel that I spent much time doing good.

That's not to say that there were not times when the positive impact of our collective efforts was not very clear and intensely inspiring. We were not merely playing at doing good, we did good.

But those moments seemed few and far between:

fund-raising and report-filing were the typical work of the day.

Yet one thing about my experience with non-profits struck me, and struck me with great surprise: they were not, as a rule, culturally fluid. The educational institutions that employed me were aware of the cultural diversity of their student and staff populations and made active efforts to smooth their interaction. Well-intended non-profit corporations (and not a few of the for-profit ones) were by no means as culturally proactive. I suppose this isn't surprising. If an area of the world hasn't enough food and water, the thing to do is get them more food and water. One doesn't need an in-depth grasp of the culture of a starving people to feed them. Nor is having a culturally diverse Board of Directors a key part of that effort.

And yet an insensitivity to that element led to a certain organizational clumsiness; an activism that was less effective than it might otherwise had been. Whenever I walked into an American schoolroom, I might well be facing an entire jumble of cultures and subcultures; but some charitable foundations I encountered were closed subcultures all their own. I sometimes felt that such organizations were vanity, an excuse for the wealthy to spread some small part of their largess in order to feel good about themselves.

I knew that was unfair: many a non-profit colleague was as idealistic and morally driven as it was possible to be. That such groups and organizations sometimes accomplished a great deal of good was certainly true; but that they embodied and lived the multiculturalism they explicitly celebrated was certainly not totally true. Nonetheless, the culture of the organizations and the cultures of those they sought to assist were often so jarringly different that those in need responded to such assistance 'from above' as insulting expressions of class arrogance or even imperialism. That class-like dissonance was often reflected even in the internal culture of organization.

That dissonance struck a chord. I began to wonder if the efforts to develop cultural tolerance and fluidity—to develop cultural competence—could be adapted from education contexts and institutions to non-educational ones. To business environments, to for-profits and non-profits. To an entire range of human organizations.

It seemed a fit subject for a dissertation.

I did a quick search of the literature. Then a deeper search. Then, I conferred with university officials. They agreed: it was indeed a worthwhile subject to explore, and such a dissertation could contribute not only to scholarly literature but enhance real-world cultural cooperation in the workplace.

I had my subject! And I got immediately down to work.

It was indeed work. The (often wonderful) distractions of teaching and non-profit charitable service were part of the reason, but the amount of study needed to ground my dissertation was at least as much a factor. It was not the writing itself so much (though mastering the tortured language of academese is a life's work in itself). It was the fact that, to make a genuinely original and non-trivial contribution to any given academic field, the author of a dissertation needs to become familiar with if not master nearly everything that has been written on a topic.

Cultural competence was not the most heavily covered subject in Academia, but it was massive enough. There were hundreds of books to pore through, thousands of articles, monographs, festschrifts. I would work all day, and read all night. As for sleep? I put an hour or so aside for that on every other weekend.

No, the labor was not small—but also not unrewarding. I felt that efforts being made in schools and educational contexts to enhance cultural tolerance and cooperation were yielding positive results. As the American people grew more multicultural, so did the American workforce, so did American organizational hierarchies. Cultural incompetence was inefficient, and in the Darwinian world of corporate competition, that was fatal. But if training in cultural competence was demonstrably effective in educational settings, I was sure similar approaches could be successfully applied in other organizational contexts—in the context of non-profit and for-profit organizations, for instance.

But I did not *know*. I could not ground it in solid fact, in sober and irrefutable data. I had to assemble all the studies that had addressed the issue, and, where they hadn't, I had to conduct my own interviews and do my own research. The current research on cultural competence and cultural competence training primarily focused on practitioners in the traditional school setting, not on those in non-school settings. This was understandable: academic researchers no doubt found it easier to examine. But what did multicultural practitioners in non-school settings experience when they attempted to develop cultural competence in their environments—if they attempted to do so at all? How did the two sets of approaches compare?

I weighed Bennett's intercultural sensitivity model—Koehn and Rosenau's superb multicultural competence paradigm—Quappe and Cantatore's cultural awareness approach. I ran semi-structured interviews with various multicultural practitioners. I coded data, compared, and critiqued studies, ran snowball samplings, conducted interviews. I read and read and read.

It was fascinating reading. Did I know when I began that mindfulness was a key to cultural competence? So it seemed. Chrobot-Mason and Leslie wrote, "Self-awareness allows the [individual] to accurately monitor and adjust his/her behavior, assumptions, stereotypes, and prejudices when dealing with [people] from various cultural backgrounds." Apparently cultural awareness involved a conscious effort to assess the effect and influence of culture not only on others but on themselves: it implied and fostered an examination of one's own cultural beliefs, one's own values and understandings of self, reality, and the world. It seemed that cultural competence involved not simply the practice of external tolerance but a journey of personal self-knowledge.

Observed Constantin, such self-examination could trigger a shift in worldview. The self-aware and culturally aware individual sees many and diverse perspectives and, in the process, opens himself or herself to new previously unknown options and cognitions. Rattanamethawong agreed: culturally aware individuals are able to explore and re-evaluate their own heritage, behaviors, beliefs; to fruitfully re-examine the values, views, and perceptions of people from their own culture as well as from other cultures.

This ability to grasp the nature of multiple cultures also allowed the culturally aware individual to grasp the similarities between cultures. It was a wonderfully valuable paradox: the more deeply one experienced a relatedness to the Other, the more awareness of that difference led to a realization of Oneness!

Quappe and Cantatore defined the levels of being culturally aware as "parochial, ethnocentric, synergistic, and participatory." The parochial are only aware of its own cultural norms. The ethnocentric recognize their cultural norms but dismiss the norms of other groups. Those at the synergistic level understand that different cultural groups may have different cultural norms, but are comfortable with an acceptance that allows for cooperation. Those at the participatory level actively work together to achieve common goals and solve common problems.

Clearly, as Dawidziuk observed—and this is of particular interest to goal-oriented organizations such as businesses and non-profits—"Individuals with tolerance for [diversity] are...more open to new information about themselves and others..." In short, those who can develop an openness to other cultures expand not only their own self-knowledge, their own cultural options, but develop a greater openness to new information as such. They develop a greater ability not just to adapt to others, but to revise their opinions in response to new data and ideas and circumstances. They become more creative, more resilient.

These hidden personal and cognitive benefits were a revelation.

The implications for peace go without saying.

Tolerance is an essential virtue for the survival and continuation of a civil democratic society. We see throughout history and all around us the fruit of the absence of tolerance—violence, terrorism, war, genocide. Yet I did not, till undertaking my research, fully understand the personal benefits of tolerance to the tolerant themselves. Tolerance was the passage from a closed and crippling mental space to a vastly larger space of personal possibilities, to a wider and deeper range of perceptions, to an unveiling of additional facts, to an expansion of mind.

Not all the voices among my reading took as positive a perspective. Intolerance, argued some, advanced group cohesion. You cannot say America First without saying Everyone Else Last! I did not agree: my love of Jamaica did not entail hatred for Mongolia. Cuba was quite different from my Jamaican home. Yet I loved visiting Cuba and wish Cuba well to this day! The German Jurist Carl Schmitt argued that fundamental to every culture was a "friend/enemy" distinction. I found that simply untrue: I did not need to make an enemy each time I made a friend. Loving one's child did not require hating some other child.

Gill, Johnstone, and Williams felt that tolerance retarded revolutionary change. At the opposite political pole from Schmitt, they followed his negative lead. They argued that "advancing emancipation and political struggle" for one group mandated oppression and political debasement of another group. I could not go along with that, either. Freeing a prisoner did not require murdering the warden. Wardens may be prisoners of the system too.

Perhaps more valuably, Aigner distinguished between "negative tolerance" and "positive tolerance." He argued that negative tolerance is a simple obliviousness to others' traditions or opinions. He considered such a tolerance unacceptable and undesirable, given the cross-cultural pluralism of modernity. There I did agree.

There were subtleties within the concept of tolerance that affected my thinking. Von Bergen's distinction between "classical" and "neoclassical" tolerance, for instance. To Von Bergen, 'classical' tolerance is simply putting up passively with disagreeable strangers; it is a quiet suffering of the Other, a peaceful but corrosively suppressed hostility. 'Neoclassical' tolerance, to Von Bergen, involved an embrace of others and their differences, without necessarily personally accepting or living those differences. Classical tolerance passively abhors; neoclassical tolerance actively and thoughtfully appreciates. In particular, it appreciates the other as a person, a fellow human being, regardless of opinion or cultural practice.

Dissent from a person's worldview, from this perspective, is not synonymous with disrespect toward the person. Such an 'authentic' (as existentialists would say) tolerance allows for the beliefs and practices of others to be questioned and critiqued but based on a healthy respect for all individuals involved—and with the condition that the person questioning the beliefs and practices of others opens himself or herself to such questioning as well. Dialogue thus becomes an open exchange, one that allows not only the articulation of one's own convictions alongside a learning about the convictions of others, but builds in both parties a heightened awareness of themselves and their cultures, as well as an openness that allows all those involved to further deepen their understanding and self-understanding. In short, to further evolve, personally and culturally.

The insights of these scholars moved me deeply. They not only enriched my understanding, but they also planted the seeds of ideas I would later develop, concepts such as cultural shadows and existential multiculturalism.

Particularly striking to me was not only what these scholars said, but what they did not say. For instance, setting up my study, I was taken by the debates of my predecessors concerning quantitative and qualitative analysis. Quantitative methods, such as questionnaires, and (culture) surveys, were valuable because of their precision, comparability, and objectivity. Qualitative methods, such as mentoring-interviews and observations, were considered valuable because of their detail, descriptiveness, and uniqueness.

Eventually I opted to include both, yet I was disturbed by the absence of something on which I could not quite put my finger. In retrospect I suppose I would call it the depth-psychological. In both quantitative and qualitative analysis, the emphasis remained on the external. Even in qualitative analysis the analyst more or less took things at face value. The working assumption was that whatever the subject reported was true (at least from the point of view of that subject), and that his or her self-knowledge and self-assessments were accurate. I had lived in America long enough to know that was quite untrue.

In no nation is racism more explicitly and repeatedly condemned; in no nation is segregation so blatant, or mutual racial animosity so universally simmering. The walls of division were as painfully obvious as the denials of that division—the sincere denials—were everywhere.

Needless to say, the data brought forth by conventional quantitative and qualitative analysis both were vast and useful, and I wanted to use and master existing tools as well as I possibly could. Nonetheless I felt it was possible to reach beyond them. I wanted to know the minds of the participants, not merely transcribe their responses.

But I stayed with convention. After all, perhaps what I wanted to reach was beyond my grasp. Skinner was right on this point: the researcher could measure behavior and responses, but not directly read minds. The value of the responses one acquired using conventional tools was certainly valuable enough.

Eventually, however, although I did stay within convention, I created models of my own—a five-part approach to cultural competence promotion; seven different ways to develop cultural competence; a paradigm involving seven obstacles that hindered cultural competence. I also defined four areas of success in developing cultural competence in groups and settings beyond the reach of traditional educational environments.

That methodology defined, I began the process of gathering data and collating results.

I will not run through that long and very arduous journey. It took several years to complete, and it was rich in insights, in anecdotes, in participant comments. I learned to appreciate as never before the thoroughness and grounding of such studies.

Suffice it to say that the goal of my study — to establish whether the approaches used in educational settings to enhance cultural skills — cultural competence — could be successfully applied in non-educational settings, was confirmed. After an examination, the academic reviewers of the document found the dissertation a valuable guide to practice.

But perhaps no reader benefitted from it more than I. I had to study the vast literature on cultural competence in academic settings and weigh and master it. As you might expect, my own cultural competence in classroom settings was greatly heightened. I had to extend the application of relevant elements of that vast literature to non-educational settings: to business environments, to non-profits, to governmental institutions and workplaces, to various formal social networks. As you might expect, my own skill set in those areas improved as well. I was able to pass along my findings, and apply those applicable in non-educational settings, with measurable and positive results, and train others to apply them as well.

What were some of my findings?

The central nature of the family was one. The most tolerant individuals, I found, were the ones whose parents and older siblings emphasized the value and practice of tolerance. That was the first 'training' such individuals received, and it was the strongest and most long-lasting.

Another was religion. A faith-based environment and community was another strong factor in cultural tolerance and cultural competence. I was struck by the comment of one participant: "The great religions are significant within a culture because... they carry the archetype at very deep unconscious levels in a culture... you can talk politics at one level, and you can talk rationally at another level, [but] unless you address those deep religious archetypes, you are really not going to move that culture." From stereotype to archetype! The comment drove me to Jung and Jungian archetypes, to considerations passing beyond psychology into psychotherapy.

Other participants were not as subtle: some were indifferent, holding that the influence of religion is declining. Still others argued that religious faith is divisive. Said another study participant, "Christianity is biased in how it looks at the rest of the world, as Islam is, as Judaism is. [They have their] worldview, [their] ideology mixed in with faith; it's very hard to deconstruct that around a common humanity."

Such was that participant's opinion, but it was not what my study found. Among the tolerant and inclusive, a faith-based element was typically present and, in many cases, explicit. The oneness of God and the oneness of humanity seemed to overlap in their thinking: the children of God might be different as individuals, but they remained siblings.

Openness to the Other in the case of the religious was not an abstract fluency: it was heartfelt, familial. True, it might have been different in earlier periods, and the historical record of religious divisiveness is as real as it is sad. In the present day, however—insofar as my study could capture it—faith and membership in faith-based communities increased cross-cultural acceptance for individuals, whereas its absence failed to do so. Disdain for God did not foster further affection for fellow human beings.

Acquiring a second language significantly increased an individual's cultural awareness and tolerance for diversity. Those who learned the language of another culture wanted to know more about that culture and were better predisposed toward individuals of that culture. More than that: they became better disposed towards other cultures in general.

Was it that mastering a second language changed their self-image—that they began to see themselves as more 'international' than parochial? Was it, as thinkers from Whorf to Wittgenstein held, that different languages contained different pictures of the world entirely? That speaking as the French speaks, say, meant thinking as the French think—that it became less the acquiring of a new skill than a cognitive expansion as such? Again, these were questions of psychology, towards which I found myself increasingly drifting.

But they were not the questions driving my study. What could improve cultural competence outside educational settings? Here was one answer. Learning the language of another culture.

I was surprised to find that celebrities loomed large when it came to enhancing tolerance and cross-cultural empathy. They appear to take on the role of brand ambassadors for their culture. (Which I personally understood. Who can listen to Bob Marley and not feel good about Jamaica?) It's hard to nurse a rabid anti-semitism and at the same time revere Marx (whether

Karl or Groucho), Woody Allen, Seinfeld, the Three Stooges. The fame of an attractive cultural representative was an extremely powerful factor in helping to make another culture as a whole attractive: the celebrity Other becomes a shorthand surrogate for the Other.

It also surprised me that many participants held strong views about the need for 'political 'will' to foster cultural harmony. I did not doubt that training in cultural fluency enhanced cultural fluency; the data showed that. A teacher so trained would handle a multicultural classroom better; a business manager so trained would handle a multicultural workforce better. Here the data were clear.

What surprised me were the comments by many participants that such training should be a core social requirement for which government bore a responsibility. One participant noted, "Barriers to cultural awareness and tolerance for diversity can be overcome through institutionalizing cultural competence, through de-institutionalizing isms, and it becoming the norm." Another observed that "There must be political will from the ground up... the kinds of circumstances and manifestations in this election cycle can't be continued."

Several of the participants felt that a strong political commitment, and the power to mobilize all the human, institutional and material resources that were needed, should be pursued; that decentralized organization and implementation by local authorities and actors were needed; that cultural competence should be an integral part of a broad national strategy designed to promote equity and justice for all.

I was not in disagreement with these sentiments. Cultural competence education "reaches far beyond the personal development of individuals, extending to communities, nations and indeed to humanity as a whole," wrote Graham and Perveen, and I certainly found that observation sound. It seemed to me that social advancement should not only enable the individual to learn and develop, but to enable societies to do so collectively.

But nowhere did I press or even articulate these as a political position. The comments arose spontaneously, which led me to suspect that one aspect of increasing cultural competence might well be an increase in evangelization among the increasingly competent.

But then I suppose I should not have been especially surprised. Enhanced cultural competence enhanced cultural interaction. It made interacting with people of other cultures more of a pleasure. Why shouldn't those enjoying that pleasure want to invite others to do so as well?

I went on to study efforts to do just that, as well as develop cultural competence in more structured terms. Cultural festivities, mass media entertainment, interpersonal dialogue and experiential opportunities such as travel, even cuisine: these were not formal training—in some cases, they were just fun. But did they support cultural interaction, cultural fluency, cultural competence? Of course. Teaching, training, assessments, and instructional modalities did too, but the notion of 'training' was intimidatingly formal. Informal cultural interaction could enhance cultural competence in ways formal drill could not.

All were effective. Yet I could not help but notice that those means that involved the joy of cultural competence seemed particularly gratifying.

It's noteworthy that participants in this study were quite open about discussing obstacles facing them while developing their cultural competence. There were internal obstacles—resistance to change; low socio-economic status; poor initial attitudes; an inclination to stereotyping; subliminal factors in interactions, such as negative or easy to misinterpret body language and unkind expressions. There were external obstacles too. Some participants had undergone cultural training before, and not every trainer was competent, nor was every training sufficient. Typically, there was lack of follow-up. Often trainings were short. Most of this stemmed from the eternal cross that all idealistic social activism has to bear: limited funding.

Yet the participants who were involved in the work of cultural competence education remained committed to that work. They believed in the transformational promise of cultural competence. They had seen it enable individuals, organizations, communities, and nations, to function better, to accomplish more—to become better human beings.

In summary? Scholarly literature was replete with attempts and evaluations of cultural competence education involving individuals who work in traditional and formal school settings.

However, and significantly, the literature lacked accounts of the experiences of multicultural practitioners who work to develop cultural competency in non-school settings. My study investigated the experiences of multicultural practitioners who work in non-school settings to develop and promote cultural competency. Importantly, the findings of this study demonstrated that efforts to develop and promote cultural competency in the academic arena could indeed be successfully mapped over into nonacademic areas, and detailed the successes experienced by participants exposed to such efforts. Limitations of the study were provided. Recommendations for further research were offered.

It was a modest but, I felt, a real and valuable addition to the scholarly literature and to our knowledge about ways to enhance cultural harmony. And for me it was a watershed.

But more importantly it led me to speculate, yet speculate realistically. I had learned how much study was needed to make a thorough and solid advance in scholarly knowledge. I had also learned how limited and time-consuming such an advance could be.

Every small fact I gathered pointed me in the direction of larger and more comprehensive syntheses, to an understanding of multiculturalism larger in sociological scope yet deeper in existential insight. I was seeking a different sort of craft, the sort of craft that could sail on larger and deeper conceptual seas.

I also felt that all the while I was serving the literature, I had been neglecting life. I had won a Doctorate, and in a modest way advanced scholarly and even practical knowledge. But had I advanced actual cultural harmony, global world peace?

Perhaps that would be asking too much, but as I thought of those grand peacemakers serving in the great conference at Caux, I realized I would need to do more, think more deeply, if I wished to truly become part of that community.

So, dissertation and Doctorate in hand, I pointed myself towards a new haven: the United Nations.

Chapter Six

The United Nations

The United Nations

The United Nations!

It felt like a miracle, a blessing. I was contemplating the many fine universities and worthy non-profit organizations and activities in the world. What to do, where to go?

I knew the answer. My eyes were cast on the United Nations. For anyone desirous of furthering the cause of world peace, it was the UN: the largest, most significant, most prestigious organization in existence dedicated to world peace. Its history was legendary, and if there was anything problematic about my aspiration, it was that the number of those wishing to join it was torrential. I knew I needed to be realistic. Any UN position to which I might aspire was probably being sought by many thousands of superbly qualified others. Who was I to be chosen among so many excellent elite competitors?

In addition, I had what I feared was a fatal demerit: I was an American citizen. Based in Manhattan, the United Nations already had a more than full complement of American members, employees, and staff. The United

Nations quite rightly aimed for representative balance, and its quota of Americans was more than likely filled.

Mind you, I did not regret becoming a citizen. Though America as a culture had its faults—or perhaps I should say its tragic and fascinating complexities—I was fully committed to America as an idea: to the concepts of democracy, of equality before the law, of freedom of speech, Constitutional and Civil rights, of representative government and personal liberty. Whatever the blemishes in its history, there was an idealism and a capacity to evolve in the American spirit that resonated with me strongly. It was a nation that wanted to better itself, and that worked to benefit others. The longer I lived here, the more that ideal spirit of America impressed me, and proved an ideal to which I chose to commit.

But (so I thought) me being a citizen wouldn't make it easier for me to get my foot in the UN door. It had probably shut it.

Even so, citizen or not, as I browsed web sites in search of academic or non-profit opportunities, I would now and then wistfully return to the UN web site and browse its application forms. I usually skipped by them, but one day I found myself musing on various wise American sayings—i.e., "What do you got to lose?" … "Aw, what's life if you don't try?" … "Go for it!"

I went for it!

I completed the online application and pressed the Send button. Days passed. Nothing happened. A week. Still no response. Two weeks. I sighed. Well, what did I expect, really?

Then one day at work—I got a call. It was from the United Nations.

I looked at the phone in disbelief.

My application had been accepted.

Acceptance was only the beginning. Joining the United Nations turned out to be a bit like joining the Army. Yes, I needed a complete physical; yes, my doctor needed to sign off on a variety of items; yes, I needed to submit any number of further documents—diplomas, resumes, national status. Yes: I needed to relocate! The United Nations is in Manhattan, and after the mild and somewhat expensive chaos that was life in Washington D. C., I found myself facing the wild and incredibly expensive chaos that was life in New York City.

(I'd thought that finding a job at the United Nations would be hard. Finding an affordable apartment in New York City—or even one single parking space—that was hard.)

But eventually I did find a place to stay, and after various enough panels inside the UN had pored over the trunkful of personal documentation I'd gathered and submitted, I was told that I would be assigned to UNESCO.

It was a logical assignment. UNESCO is the educational arm of the United Nations, and I had, after all, been teaching for several years now. I had written and lectured and published on the subject of education, I had worked as a school administrator, I had trained teachers. My professional training and academic qualifications revolved around Education. The match seemed perfect.

I remember the day I arrived at the UN, seeing the lines of its classic, world-renowned architecture rising into the bright clouds over New York. It was amazing, exhilarating, inspirational. I felt as though I were in Cuba again, dumbfounded at the sheer iconic beauty of that edifice. I walked up its steps for the first time aching to enter its corridors, passionate to begin my work.

Work that turned out to be... surprising. I was not quite sure what I was expecting, but I assumed the research work would be something along the lines of my dissertation research, and the teaching or training, if any, would involve actual classroom teaching or teacher training.

Instead, I found myself attending a tremendous number of meetings and then being asked to summarize and/or synthesize what had been said. Occasionally I would be asked to do secondary research, fact-check, collate data from multiple sources, supply an official or sub-agency with information about some education-related subject, and pass the results along in a report.

So mostly I did a great deal of attending meetings, observing, reporting, reading and writing. Much of it was of a contemporary nature and could involve some pressing crisis or some more chronic matter.

At times it was quite disheartening. For instance, I learned at one presentation that almost sixty million children of primary school age had never attended school. Sixty million! I thought of how much reading books had meant to me personally, of how much I'd gained from attending school and the opportunities I've been afforded. Walking the streets of New York under the world-famous luxury logos and by the universally known brand name Banks with their implication of wealth without limit, it was painful to reflect that elsewhere sixty million children — including young people, about two hundred and sixty million in total, over a quarter of a billion global youth—were being left to live lives intellectually maimed by being excluded from education. An endless vista of children, capable of contributing so much, cast aside.

Yet the data I collated could be inspiring, too. Once, almost 99% of humanity could not read. Now 95% of humanity could. There was no question as to where humankind was headed, thanks to the educational efforts of groups such as the United Nations. No, progress was not an illusion but a reality. Together the nations of the world had gone far towards relieving many ills. There was only a little further to go.

To an outsider, the many talks and assemblies at the UN are sometimes made to look long-winded and not very effective, but I quickly learned better. It was my task to ground all the aspirations and their results in hard data, so I knew full well about how daunting were the problems it faced, and about all the good that the organization did regardless. It was inspiring to see, and well worth gathering data to make it better known.

It was work I did in the background, and so long as I could do it, I was content. The meetings and conferences which I attended were sometimes extremely high-level, and often I would attend them in the company of a notable UNESCO official, to whom I would hand summaries or talking points for their presentation.

My supervisor was the one with the authority to speak on behalf of UNESCO. I was there to do the good, humble work of a foot soldier, and so long as my work was helping advance the goals of the United Nations even in that small way, I was happy.

Nonetheless, after, a while, I would find myself walking down the corridors of the United Nations and Ambassadors and representatives from Ghana or Mexico or France would give me a wave.

"Doctor Vernon. How nice to see you."

"It's my pleasure entirely, Ambassador."

"Would you like to join me for lunch?"

"Well, I—thank you, yes."

And over such lunches and dinners and casual connections my true education in the United Nations and intercultural diplomacy began.

Please do not imagine that I am making more of my place or my influence than it truly was. I was there to research, to collate and synthesize literature, and to write, and to do all of this in support of officials handling the official business of UNESCO. My role was supportive, and the only thing more that I can say is that I loved, dearly, the noble and necessary goals for which UNESCO labored and fought. I was happy to serve in however a category I could.

But at the same time, an evolution was taking place inside of me. It was the fact of simply being there, in that environment. These were the people actively building world peace, actively striving to deconstruct outdated animosities between emerging nations and between those nations and the superpowers, actively seeking to peacefully supersede the old orders of colonialism and imperialism and replace them with a new and beneficial order of world peace. I shared their aspirations, but I was no longer a distant outsider looking in. Humble as my part was, I was one of them now.

At Caux, I had been a teenager looking up to strong,

mature, powerful figures who, for me, embodied experiential wisdom and moral leadership. Now I was trained and had some measure of expertise in a relevant field, I was much the same age as many others there, and while I was officially there to record the representatives' views, increasingly the representatives were asking for mine.

It was intoxicating, humbling, and at the same time oddly prosaic. A diplomat from Great Britain did in fact ask me to lunch. We sat and chatted! First about education, then about Jamaica and England, then about life at the UN, then about—well, the minor personal things people chat about. It was completely casual, and yet not. I had a Doctorate in Education and had written a dissertation on Cultural Competence. People who cared about those subjects wanted to pick my brain. What was so surprising about that?

I slowly began to realize that it was in such side events as these that so much actually gets accomplished. One imagines that it is only at official gatherings that decisions are made, and actions are taken. It may well be that it is at such gatherings that decisions and actions are finalized and made official, but what I learned at the UN is that it is in private dialogues and personal conversations that formal facades are removed, and official stances replaced with truer expressions; that it is at such moments that diplomatic roles are put aside in exchange for those existential moments that truths are spoken.

"Speak Truth To Power" is a noble maxim, and in my capacity as an educator I sought to do exactly that. But at these side events, these unexpected personal encounters,

I found myself witnessing Power itself speaking Truth to Power.

It was strangely compelling, for I found that some of the most powerful, well-known, and most influential of figures were in fact quite decent and well-intentioned individuals who were as uncertain and unsure of what to do next as the person in the street. They too were groping for a better world, but groping in a strange new darkness, where the explosion of information had grown too large to be meaningfully ingested, and the rate of historical and technological change had accelerated to such a pace that the ground of world society seemed to change radically each new time one set foot upon it.

Their good will was as palpable as it had been at Caux. Yet good will alone was not enough. They grappled with the sorrows and the challenges of the world in good conscience. But did good conscience alone provide solutions? If not, what would? How to better understand the world, so as to better heal it?

The situation required, to coin a phrase I found myself using more and more often, "further analysis." After many a day's work, I would go home and begin making notes; notes and thoughts about just that, subjects I discuss in the next three chapters.

The United Nations was not Caux, though I knew that my youthful idealism may have colored that earlier experience. There was far more bureaucratization. There were certain department heads who seemed to feel that to work for peace and to generate paperwork was the same thing. Nor was the wish for a better world always universal. Most UN personnel and officials did indeed seem animated by that wish, but there were member nations and people associated with them that were quite nationalistic and parochial.

For a very few, the UN was a battleground, a "War of All against All," as Thomas Hobbes put it, where the task of each day was denunciation of perceived enemies, not cooperation between equals. Yet those voices were valuable too. Peace needs to be built in the real world under real conditions involving real people. Idealism must learn to acknowledge and accommodate the non-idealistic and competing idealisms. Dissent could be a contribution as well.

Such contributions tended to be more vivid and honest—and sometimes were admittedly conceded to be only official posturing—in personal exchangea. That was yet another thing that made an occasional casual lunch so valuable.

Such side events were not always small or intimate—quite the contrary. One day, on my way to deliver a report, a delegation from the Dominican Republic encountered me in the halls. They began asking questions out of the blue about some educational matters. I answered, and one of the delegates invited me on the spot to be the Keynote Speaker at an upcoming seminar they had already scheduled. I said yes, of course, and imagined I would be addressing a small classroom. Upon arriving, the 'tiny seminar' was a massive symposium of scores of individuals from an entire range of Embassies.

They had invited me because they wanted an expert discussion concerning intercultural education. Ease of travel, increased immigration and a borderless internet meant that virtually every nation's educational institutions had to accommodate multiple cultures now, especially nations that were effectively 'supercultures,' (a term I had privately come up with for sprawling multicultural entities like the United States where everything was at once vividly American yet one ethnic neighborhood could be a different cultural universe from the one on the next street down).

I shared my views, albeit verbally improvising rather like a Jazz performer. Then—another surprise—the room was thrown open to questions, and guest after guest asked my views on this educational subject and that. Discussion was long and informal and seemed to range over everything, and afterwards representatives from still other delegations gave me further invitations to speak.

It was humbling. Yet the truth was, I was mostly grateful not for the chance to speak, but for the many opportunities to listen. Such informal talks and lunches and appearances was often where the real thinking was done and the eventual consensus hammered out. There was a depth and significance to the unofficial United Nations, its internal community, that was quite as important and significant as its formal pronouncements. Reading the American press, I would smile at the phrase, 'Deep State,' with its conspiratorial connotations. There was no Deep State at the United Nations, yet there was indeed a kind of 'Deep Community' among officialdom and their satellites interacting with the satellites of other representatives assembled there. There was nothing conspiratorial about it, only an evolving shared sensibility, a gradually shared agreement about what mattered more and what mattered less, about what needed immediate attention and what didn't, about what was possible and what was not. This consensus was not arrived at during high public debate, although public debate and official proclamation might confirm it. The consensus formed itself off to the side, in relative privacy.

That did not make it any the less thoughtful or informed or sincere. Rather the contrary. In 'side events,' the unspoken could be spoken, the sensitive plainly addressed. Nor was that 'relative privacy' always private. Consciousness could be raised in unofficial forums and gatherings and seminars that were quite public, and quite powerful.

I mentioned earlier a session on global education. The actual occasion was the presentation of a global education monitoring report hosted and published by UNESCO. I was neither the researcher nor a speaker, only a participant. Yet as I listened, I felt myself becoming immersed in the sheer cataracts of data, crushing data about world illiteracy and the lack of access of hundreds of millions of young—hundreds of millions—to any sort of schooling at all. The depth of the presentation was astounding and depressing to hear when it came to the contrast between the poorest and most marginalized nations and peoples and the wealthiest and most privileged.

As a teacher myself in one of the wealthiest and most privileged of nations, America, I remembered with a kind of pain seeing students sitting in classes flipping through their smartphones, concerned less with their educational opportunities than with their tattoos and clothes and sneakers. One shook one's head. Some had so much, and others so little, and those who had so much did not even care.

I left the session both inspired and half in despair. Illiteracy was close to being globally erased. Thanks to the internet, even the poorest now had access to the highest peaks of world culture and to immense educational resources—yet with such a gift in their hands, so many preferred to use it to access game and hate sites.

I thought again, not for the first time, about the need for moral education, for training not merely in informational access but in existential sensibility. No poll was taken, but as I looked across at other faces from other lands and cultures, I knew many of the other participants in the seminar felt the same. It was not a formal policy statement, only a shared unspoken sentiment. Yet it was precisely such shared unspoken sentiments that underpinned so much of what the UN did.

Another of such transformative side events was a seminar I attended at the United Nations on the global culture of peace. Again, I was only a participant, but what an intellectual and spiritual feast it was. That gathering was truly a resurrection and extension of the spirit of Caux. There were representatives from the Holy See, Tibetans, Imams, priests and monks and others decked out in full religious regalia, resonant with their faith yet transcending difference and ideologies in their common search for peace. And beside them, scholars of world stature—I remember one German scholar whose talk on hermeneutics and exilic literature I would not call an intellectual feast, but a full course of gourmet intellectual cuisine!

All of it highlighted what my dissertation had proven—the immense importance of the religious community in promoting a culture of peace.

However grim the data UN officials might encounter elsewhere, sessions such as these left them inspired once more. I know that nothing so re-ignited my own passion for peace as much as hours like these.

No less transformative, though daunting, were frequent presentations on climate change. Data about the planet, the weather patterns, geological and atmospheric changes would be presented that raised the stark question of human survivability. Could our species, could any species, survive the worst possible scenarios that some scientists were projecting? What could we do to bring the world back from extinction? What did it portend even if we did survive?

I remember the Prime Minister of one island State who gave a moving presentation and made a passionate plea. Her homeland was literally sinking. Every year the water level rose, and projections confirmed that the land where her people had lived throughout all known history would one day simply be covered over by the sea and vanish. What would her people do? Where would they go?

And what would happen when they got there? What about the changes to those places? Climate Change changed demographics and migration patterns too. Did this portend a new age of population displacement? Did that portend a new age of neo-nationalist resentment and pushback, of ethnonationalist autarky? What would that do to the global economy, to existing power relations and current social landscapes? How could the United

Nations and its programs and policies help member nations survive these coming disruptions—assuming the world could survive them at all?

The answer to that would require a good deal of thought.

We share our world with nearly eight billion people. Soon there will be nine billion of us, all wanting a good, just, and peaceful quality of life. Can we meet human needs without destroying the ecological systems and exhausting the natural resources on which our civilization depends?

The UN had indeed proved an extension of Caux. Here at the UN were the movers and the shakers, the actual framers of policy, actively shaping the decisions and future directions of their nations and their cultures.

But I gradually came to see that, for all the informational splendor of its many forums and seminars, and for all the good and charitable policies it undertook, it was the intellectual element that led in importance. The longer I looked at the world, the more I saw new problems and circumstances to which the old approaches and solutions did not apply or applied with decreasing effectiveness. Reassessments and new solutions were needed. I did not delude myself that I had all the answers, but my reflections—some of which I present in the next three chapters—seemed to me to point out at least a few valuable new directions. It would take more than one person to explore them all in their full depth; my efforts were only a pointing of the way. But if I never sat down and put them into a book, they might never get explored at all.

During my tenure at the United Nations, I slowly

became aware of a phenomenon that filled me with interest—and, increasingly, with concern. We are all very much aware of it: the internet. In those days, during its beginnings, it was not remotely as overwhelming as it is now. The internet back then was a set of glowing orange and green lines of text on what looked like a small television with a keyboard. It kept records and allowed you to type without having to make corrections on paper. How nice! Then, it turned out to be capable of sending messages over the wires. Even better! How could our attitudes toward that be anything but entirely positive? Rapid international communication became possible. We could communicate by phone, of course, but internet email cost nothing to send or receive. It facilitated communication, and we welcomed it.

But then came sound files. And images. And then moving images. And then Live Chat. And then online communities—forums and wikis, Facebooks and Reddits. Then video calls—Skype and Zoom. What had begun as an exchange of comments via computer had become a fully immersive experience. And with that my interest in cultural communications took an extraordinary and, I believe, original turn.

I also became fascinated with other such subjects—subjects of deep importance to the understanding of cultures and cultural harmony, yet areas of thought that were in themselves 'side events'—areas that had caught the glancing attention of some scholars, yet not enough sufficient attention to bring their importance to full public consciousness.

For instance, I began exploring, not the psychology of cultures, but the application of various psychotherapies to cultures, the transposition of techniques proven effective for individuals to greater social wholes.

I began thinking as well of what marked those individuals who had truly made a difference to world peace and social justice—the Ashokas, the Tolstoys, the Mahatma Gandhis, the Dalai Lamas, the Rabins and Sadats, the Mandelas, the many rightful recipients of the Nobel Peace Prize. Examining their commitment and their passion, I began to perceive the outlines of an *existential* multiculturalism, a multiculturalism not of grudging or indifferent endurance of the Other, but of activity, of like commitment, of mindful awareness—a multiculturalism of the Spirit. I began to think of the social content of that social and intellectual standpoint, which is to say: of Utopia.

My time at the UN was one of the most significant and satisfying times in my life. I left deeply committed to playing my part—to educate in values with a view to changing the social consciousness of our global citizens and to educate for a culture of peace, non-violence, tolerance, and respect. I cannot think of more important work to do, or a finer or more necessary organization than the United Nations in which to do it.

But my term at the UN was nearly complete. There were personal affairs needing my attention as well, not least and the need to finally assemble my thoughts and reflections into a book—this book.

It was time to go.

Part Two

*New
Perspectives*

Chapter Seven

Cultural Shadows

Cultural Shadows

Writing my dissertation was a joy. I sank into hundreds of papers and journals and books with complete abandon.

A doctoral dissertation is intended to accomplish several tasks: one is to demonstrate complete familiarity with the literature on a subject; another is to further add one's own original contribution to that literature. It need not be world-shaking, and most dissertations are not intended to revolutionize the subject. Neither was mine. My goal was modest, though, I felt, substantive: I wanted to demonstrate beyond any reasonable doubt that academic training in multicultural fluidity which had already been proven effective in academic settings could be fruitfully applied to non-academic organizational settings; that it could be fruitfully adapted to business or NGO or military or other organizational environments.

That notion seemed to me a reasonable belief. My dissertation had put it on a solid footing, I believed, and the dissertation committee agreed.

But even as I was writing it, I had a suspicion that I was

mastering a literature of the past. Valid and admirable material to be sure! Material that would always be worth considering and perspectives that would always be worth re-visiting. But still material that addressed a subject that was changing, virtually mutating, even as I was examining it.

I do not use the word 'virtually' lightly. Nor the word 'mutating'. When I first arrived in America, I had a very clear focus: I wanted to study living cultures to see how they could better harmonize—ideally, one day, to help foster peace between all cultures. The end goal was large, but the means I explored were practical and measurable, with foundations that were empirical and descriptive.

Yet as I rose though American academia, I found that cultural studies as I had known them had been largely overshadowed in academia in favor of a novel *doppelgänger* that was also called 'Cultural Studies,' but was something quite different. This new version of 'Cultural Studies' seemed driven by something called Theory, a nebulous descendant of Critical Theory, which was itself a hybrid offspring of a body of thought called Deconstruction mixed with a good helping of Foucault and various flavors of Western Marxism that had its roots in the Frankfurt School.

These 'Cultural Studies' were not studies or descriptions of cultures so much as writings that took some given cultural phenomenon, passed it through a sausage-grinder of French and European philosophical terminology, and used what emerged to assert that, say, gender did not exist, but that 'male' and 'female' were social constructs built to serve the obscured oppressive weight of Capital. All human relations under Capitalism were relations of power, and all cultural artifacts under that system, even apparently biological characteristics like race or gender, were deceptive masks of oppressive Capital.

Many of the writers—Derrida, Deleuze, Foucault, Cornel West, Judith Butler, Marcuse, Lacan, Mouffe, Negri, Zizek—were interesting and thought-provoking, even powerful. But frankly, I often felt myself to be wading through a fog of words that had little practical application. The goal in these texts always seemed to be Revolution, though how it would come about was obscure. After it did, something very positive would happen, though it was hard to make out exactly what.

Was this an advance on the older, less theoretical work I had studied— the writings of actual real-life peacemakers like Gandhi and Martin Luther King, of students of culture such as Ruth Benedict or Marvin Harris or Max Weber, or even philosopher-historians like Spengler or Gibbons, Hegel, and Carlyle—or was it a strange and cryptic turn onto a wrong road? The most interesting thing about this academic movement concerning culture, to me, was the fact that it seemed to have produced an academic subculture all its own, with its own journals, departments, mutual citations, code words, private language and (he)gemonic (con)ferences. Frankly it was more interesting as a social phenomenon than what it said about social phenomena.

But encountering it had the positive effect of driving me ever deeper into the empirical. What I wanted to know, after all, was really very simple. How can we stop Israelis and Palestinians (say) from bombing one another? How cab even just reduce the amount of bombing, and foster a better relationship? Convincing the parties involved in such conflicts that they had no gender and/or 58 different genders because of racial hatred between races that were also non-existent social constructs engineered by Capitalism—well, that just didn't look like it would really help. Indeed, it seemed to me that falling into what often seemed self-referential intellectual language games only served to distract well-intended and intelligent minds from helping.

What concrete incremental steps could we take to reduce the antagonism between antagonistic cultures, to foster some degree of real and measurable improvement? Surely there were some. Seeing the direction that this new fashion in Cultural Studies was taking dismayed me, for it seemed to me to be displacing that question. But that dismay bore fruit: it tore me farther and farther away from abstractions and drove me to look at cultures today as they 'live and move and have their being' in the real world, and not as reinterpreted by Marxist academicians.

And yet—did they have a point? Were the nineteenth and twentieth century models I had been studying still valid?

What were cultures like in the modern world, and how were they operating now, in modern circumstances? There will always be value in earlier observations, and there are certainly sound and unexpected insights among newer cultural thinkers. But when I looked away from theory and directly at culture as it seemed to be operating at present, I found there were characteristics— one major development in particular—that both the old schools and the new missed. Something new had arrived on the scene, and it was not theoretical, but practical in the most serious sense.

I contend that there has been a fundamental change in cultures and cultural relations since the beginning of the twenty-first century—indeed, a fundamental change on every level in the way human beings relate to one another.

That change involves the internet. Or to be precise, the degree of usage of the internet. Because of that change, most human beings no longer interact the way they have interacted throughout all previous human history, nor do they interact in the way they have been designed by evolution to interact. The way we are trying to interact now because of that change in media may make it ultimately impossible for us to interact successfully at all. The implications of which are—unknown.

Perhaps I can make my idea clearer by placing it in a larger context, contrasting the present-day situation to the past.

Throughout the vast majority of our existence as a species, human beings and human society have dealt with each other directly, face-to-face, in limited geographical areas. As hunter-gatherers, wandering in small tribes, human beings existed and interacted with one another in small communities. From these close and intimate interactions, shared customary behaviors and beliefs—cultures—arose. Eventually grand and extended cultures. But still cultures rooted in the context of direct inter-personal relations, tribal rituals, idiosyncratic customs, among extended families of small but coherent groups. Their interactions were immediate, and the cultures that arose were informed by that immediacy. Their culture and their lived experience were one—their culture was the equivalent to their lived experience.

Cultures were local and regional—indeed, there are evolutionary psychologists who contend that cultures were so localized to particular regions for so long that the individuality of those cultures led even to a degree of biological individuality, to the beginnings of different and distinct evolutionary paths.

Tribal conquests did occur, and mass migrations. The more powerful tribe would drive out, or absorb, the weaker one, and the victor's culture remain coherent and persist, changing only very slowly over time. Eventually those small tribes and wandering groups settled and grew into towns and villages, and eventually into city-states. Some grew so large that they were able to host smaller different segregated cultures within themselves, under their territorial control.

But not until very recently, in the past few thousand years, have institutions and technology grown to the point where a culture could extend much beyond the physical reality of its geographical boundaries, and thus its base of immediate, face-to-face, personal social interaction. Books and newsprint were a cataclysmic development—suddenly, the thoughts and stories of a culture could be preserved, and the thoughts and stories of different cultures shared; even shared globally.

But only the statistically tiny groups that were literate, the small and educated elite, could experience them. Most people remained in their historical regions, and the vast majority, illiterate, had only vague ideas about distant cultures and different ways of life. Human societies and social interaction continued to be what millennia of evolution had shaped them to be: direct, immediate, aural, tactile, person-to-person.

This began to change slowly in the beginnings of the modern age, with the arrival of ships and then railroads, and then radically in the twentieth century with the arrival of radio and television. People of various cultures suddenly became self-aware to a never-before-experienced degree and began to interact with people of other cultures.

With the arrival of the internet that encounter became a flood. A flood that, I will argue, is turning inwards upon itself in strange and unexpected ways.

The *coup de grace* occurred in 1993.

In November 1992, there were no more than twenty-six websites in the world. While there were obscure predecessors, not easy to use or access, there was nothing similar to a web browser as we know it today.

Then, in 1993, Mosaic 2.0 was released. It was the first user-friendly browser, and the first genuinely popular one, with an attractive graphic interface easy for non-programmers to install.

Access to the Internet soon exploded far beyond the limits of technical specialists and military-industrial institutions.

By August 1995 the twenty-six sites in existence earlier had burgeoned to over 10,000.

By 1998 the number was in the millions.

By 2019, over half the people on the world—53.6%—were online. In the developed world, that number was 86.6%.

Today? According to Wikipedia, in a world with

over seven billion people, over five billion people are internet users. And the unprecedented explosion in usage continues: a rule of thumb called Edholm's Law tells us that internet bandwidth in telecommunications networks continues to double every 18 months.

How long are we online or in front of digitized screens now, interacting digitally via the net instead of physically, in person—watching, some would say, rather than living? In America, people now spend their time gazing into screens for over eleven hours a day—most of our waking life. In North America, the average person spends over two hours on social media alone. In Africa, over three hours. In South America the number is approaching four.

The Bureau of Labor Statistics tells us that we spend one year and eleven months of our lives directly socializing with our fellow human beings. But that we spend nearly seven years of our lives socializing on social media.

Stop for a moment and let that number sink in. We now spend roughly four times as much time interacting with people online than we do socializing with them in person. And these statistics are before the pandemic, after which workplaces across the world became digital, not physical, and lockdowns and social distancing drove people even further into private cocoons whose only window onto most other human beings is the internet.

What are the psychological effects of this transition from immediate interaction with others to computer-mediated interaction? Notes World Psychiatry," the official journal of the World Psychiatric Association:

"...unique features of the online world may be influencing: a) attentional capacities, as the constantly evolving stream of online information encourages our divided attention across multiple media sources, at the expense of sustained concentration; b) memory processes, as this vast and ubiquitous source of online information begins to shift the way we retrieve, store, and even value knowledge; and c) social cognition, as the ability for online social settings to resemble and evoke real-world social processes creates a new interplay between the Internet and our social lives, including our self-concepts and self-esteem."

It concludes that, "Overall, the available evidence indicates that the Internet can produce both acute and sustained alterations in each of these areas of cognition, which may be reflected in changes in the brain."

That the way we live now is making unknown yet literal changes in humanity's physical brains, and doing so globally, is daunting. But it is not my subject. I am concerned here only with cultures and how cultures interact in the context of peace or aggression. How does this "new interplay between the Internet and our social lives" play out culturally?

You would imagine that the result would be positive—that it would foster amalgamation. With all the regions, religions, races, all the age groups and genders and ethnicities now drawn constantly into the vortex of the internet, surely you would think that we have bid the world of nationalism and ethnic separatism goodbye, and taken up happy residence full- time in McLuhan's global village. Surely now that we live online most of our waking day, spending our time in a world without borders, all the various cultures must be melding at last into one world culture, a vast cognitive melting pot intermingling each into all.

You would be mistaken.

Watching friends from different cultures interact with others on the web, I began to get an inkling of something novel happening—a significant social phenomenon that I could not yet quite name. I came across it by observing the sad decline of several friends into political polarization—extreme, acrid, deeply emotional, polarization.

In my debates in Jamaica as a young man, different positions on various topics might be held, and held quite passionately. Debate could be heated, even intemperate. But whatever the subject, at the end the day, the debaters remained friends. Our attitudes were rather like the reported comment of Pope John XXIII to the Communist Mayor of Rome during a walk together. "After all, what separates us? Only our opinions. You must admit that that's not very much."

That was how we felt. We might disagree, but so what? We had a common humanity. That transcended any differences. That was simply a given.

Yet in America, during the candidacy of Donald Trump, I saw political disagreement mutate overnight into visceral hatred. Whichever side you were on, anyone on the opposite side was regarded as vermin. It was shocking. No one merely agreed or disagreed with Trump or his policies in a calm and detached way: one either idolized him or despised him (in the academic world, typically the latter), and those who dissented were ostracized and shunned, detestable moral lepers. They were no longer—and this was the daunting cultural element—'one of us.'

To one side, Trump was a Nazi, a bigot, a racist, a xenophobe, a mobster, a rapist, a conscious Russian stooge! If you happened to favor Trump, you were not merely honestly mistaken. Your support was tantamount to conscious Holocaust denial or child molestation. Of course, Trump's followers like Trump himself were far from temperate in their responses to his accusers, and the virulent cult-like absurdity of Qanon conspiracies were lunacies all their own.

But what surprised me—what shocked me—was not just the sheer livid dehumanizing intensity of both sides, but their completely opposed reports about what ought to have been indifferent and palpable social facts. Both sides seemed to hold two completely opposed images of current political events in their heads. They seemed to be living in two entirely different parallel worlds.

Slowly I began to realize that while they might be living in one shared real world, both existed in two very different media environments. The Trump supporter would get all his news and opinions from the New York Post, Fox News, Rush Limbaugh. Those who despised Trump got all their information from the New York Times, National Public Radio, CNN.

The two might socialize professionally, even personally, though with deteriorating frequency and politeness. But as I read their email or encountered them on internet forums and online, as time and again I saw the language of both sides grow swiftly and viciously more intemperate, I noticed that each side began more and more restricting themselves to their own closed online networks. The discussion groups each attended, the lists of followers and those Friended and Unfriended, became more polarized by the day. Cancellation became the informal norm. If you disagreed with the group consensus, whatever its consensus, you were 'downvoted' on sites like Reddit, or deplatformed or demonetized on YouTube, or increasingly, simply banned outright. Sometimes with offline consequences, such as job loss.

I soon noticed that the cultural correlates of either side were similarly polarized. Few Trump supporters listened to Rap; few Trumpophobes enjoyed Country. Some Trump supporters hunted for sport; few Trumpophobes hunted. Nearly all Trumpophobes spent part of their free time engaged in social activism—they donated to the ACLU, supported climate change, attended rallies for gay or women's rights; Trump supporters watched wrestling, or spent time playing violent video games.

I realized what I was looking at was not the unrelated disconnected actions of discrete individuals, but the behaviors of a new and different sort of cultural phenomenon--a new and different sort of *culture*. And once I saw it, I began to see it elsewhere, almost everywhere. African Americans had a subculture all their own online on "Black Twitter." China had a Chinese internet community that was policed and all but quasi-segregated from the rest of the internet. Young girls flocked to TikTok. Young boys (if neo-Nazi) could be found infesting boards like /pol/ on 4chan.

These cultures and subcultures were not merging into a global village— rather, they were carving out a part of the internet and half-unconsciously, half-intentionally segregating themselves, forming an online community where like meets like, crystallizing their subcultures and repelling difference. They were real individuals living lives in the real world, often highly disconnected from one another in that real world, yet at the same time they had created a reflection of their cultural world on the internet. And that is where most of their cultural interactions seemed to be taking place.

Soon I observed that not only subcultures were doing this. To some degree all cultures were.

And at this point I began to form my ideas about cultural shadows.

What is a 'cultural shadow'?

A cultural shadow is the online expression of an offline, real, and living culture.

It may be the expression of a small subculture, like the online community of an offline fringe group. It may be the expression of a far wider subculture, like the collective internet outpourings of a specific age group or ethnic minority. It may be the collective dialogues of a major cultural entity, like the sprawling online network of Facebook considered as a collective entity, different but common in their submission to Facebook protocols or posting guidelines. It may be a top-down template shaping cultural expression like the internet of China when the State both mandates access and excises material deemed unsuitable. It may be a political subculture, like the digitally networked communities of Islamic radicalism or white nationalism. It may be, to a degree, nationally enclosed, like the online Russian or Japanese internet communities. Participants may overlap: those active in one online or offline real or culture may participate in others as well.

But all cultural shadows have a few basic things in common:

Like shadows, they are the expression of and follow a living offline culture.

Like shadows, they are the distorted expression of that culture. The online expressions may mirror discussions in the underlying culture, but often present them in cut-down or exaggerated or 'edgy' or extreme forms.

Like shadows, they are blanker than the culture that produces them. The whole of a culture does not and cannot express itself in Tweets and Upvotes and Likes: much is said, but much is unsaid.

Like shadows, they accompany the figures that casts them in real time. If a crisis or even a subject of trivial significance catches the attention of a real-life community, its online shadow reflects that concern and how the culture conceptualizes it and feels about it immediately, at once, as the event occurs and so long as it keeps occurring.

And vice versa. For there is one major difference between physical and cultural shadows. Unlike physical shadows, cultural shadows modify the cultures that cast them. The tropes and memes and cultural emanations that make up the cultural shadow turn around and influence and reshape the underlying real culture that produces them.

Like a scenario for an episode of The Twilight Zone, our cultural shadows are now casting us!

This is not just a rhetorical figure. If people now spend over four times as much of their lives interacting with each other through social media than socializing with each other in real life, the main source of the cultural changes that such exchanges produce must shift to the internet. If so, as McLuhan said, "the medium is the message": and if the medium intrinsically distorts the message, it inevitably distorts the culture underlying it.

In what way? We already have evidence of the ease with which online communities trend in disturbing directions:

Information deformity—witness the way pro- and anti-vaccination forces ignore or dismiss evidence counter to their positions while emphasizing or spreading debatable evidence, provided it supports their own.

Mass polarization—witness the increasing division worldwide as the consensus of online group opinion increasingly becomes the marker of group membership.

Extremist radicalization—witness the clear link established by antiterrorism experts between fringe online media consumption and the statistical likelihood of terrorist activity, and how that fringe rhetoric seeps into mainstream discourse.

Digital mob rule—witness the phenomenon of "doxxing' or 'cancellation,' where individuals who oppose or break with the digital group consensus are expelled, deplatformed, demonetized, effectively silenced, even targeted for real life harassment.

This is more than saying that the online image of a people (or that the online image projected by a people, intentionally or unintentionally) is not always an accurate image. Of course, it isn't: it isn't intended to be. For the most part it's a spontaneous collage of ever-moving dialogues, like a kaleidoscopic frieze of emails from a billion smartphones changing from moment to moment.

But as the old IBM adage had it: "Information overload equals pattern recognition." When there is too much information to take in, the mind simplifies what it sees. What begins as expression and returns as reflection collapses into stereotype.

What results is a kind of cocooning—not the cocooning coined in 1981 by the prophetic marketing consultant Faith Popcorn, the decision to stay "inside one's home, insulated from danger, instead of going out." This new cocooning consists of a culture's inclination to wrap around itself only those media sources that reflect its preferred image of itself and the world—for example, the inclination of right-wing culture to access only right-wing news sites and blogs and forums, and the inclination of left-wing culture to access only left-wing news sites and blogs and forums.

These are sharpened examples of the inclination of all cultures today to wrap a particular digital environment about themselves and convince themselves that what they are seeing is the world and themselves as they are, when in reality they are only seeing a complex yet over-simplified digital simulacra, interpretations of the world and themselves as they prefer yet also believe the world and themselves to be.

All cultural shadows have this same quasi-reality: they are not wholly false, but they are sufficiently selective about those things to which they attend that the world and the sense of cultural self that appears to them is a skein of fawning interpretations. When that online image, those interpretations, are widely enough accepted and repeated by a culture, they permeate the culture, they become the culture—or rather, they push the culture into becoming a dysfunctional version of itself, a culture that has stepped away from the face-to-face street level of real world interaction to the virtual level of, yes, a 'social construct,' a presence that is at the same time an absence.

The real-world results can be dire. For instance, apparent corruption in the gaming industry led to an explosion of online discussion in the online gaming community. The scandal, called 'Gamergate,' is widely considered to be the spark that led to the emergence of the Alt-Right, a dissident far- right faction whose online presence was a significant influence in the election of Donald Trump in 2016, and which even now exerts a gravitic force in conservative American politics.

The aim of revolutionary Marxist politics was to gain control of the means of production; the aim of contemporary revolutionary politics seems to be to gain dominant market share over the means of communications. If war, as Clausewitz said, is politics conducted by other means, war is now politics conducted by other memes. The implications for peace studies are unsettling.

One thinks of the French media philosopher

Baudrillard and his notorious trio of articles, *The Gulf War Did Not Take Place*. In those articles Baudrillard argued that, yes, the events and violence of the Gulf War did take place, but that what was not what really mattered. What mattered was what was presented concerning the War over global media. The spectacle and the interpretations about what happened took effective priority over what did take place. To those in the shade of American cultural shadows, the War On Terror took place to Make The World Safe For Democracy, and those shadow phenomena are what actually 'happened.' The bodies were mere incidentals. The battle for dominance by the conflicting cultural narratives was the real battle.

That ambiguity has only grown. Was the Coronavirus pandemic one of the greatest plagues ever to afflict the world, or was it a hoax? Was 9/11 planned and executed by Islamic radicals, or the CIA? If the Gulf War did not take place, what about the Holocaust?

Make no mistake: the Gulf War, Coronavirus fatalities, 9/11 and the Holocaust did take place. But if we take our notions of historical truth mainly from web sites motivated by different cultural special interests, we end up with what is in every sense a clash of unrealities — of distorted shadows.

It may be objected that what I call 'cultural shadows' are hardly a new phenomenon. There have always been cultural images cast by cultures: for instance, the idea of Victorian culture in books has always had a somewhat independent existence from its reality. Our generally accepted picture of Victorianism has been constructed from the dominant media of that time, print. That image has been drawn brightly by Charles Dickens and other

Victorian novelists or sketched darkly by Friedrich Engels in *The Condition Of The Working Class In England*. There too, those depictions of Victorian culture surely had reciprocal effects on the actual underlying culture.

But there is a difference between books appearing some years after the fact among a minority of literate readers, and immediate participation in real time by most of the people making up the actual underlying culture. When most daily cultural interaction are onscreen, and nearly everyone in the world is on social media four hours a day, and watching those screens eleven hours a day, then, as Marx observed, quantity changes quality: enough of a quantitative change has passed the threshold to produce a change in the very quality of a culture as a whole.

Cognitive market share online is not the same as concrete realities offline, of course; if it were, the largest nation in the world would be Google. Actually existing cultural relations, actually existing means of handling cultural relations such as negotiation and diplomacy between existing nations and groups and institutions, still persist.

Nonetheless, the implications of most of the world spending most of their time online has major implications for the very meaning of culture as we see and understand it today. The implications for cultural study—and peace between different cultures—are, at minimum, radically altered.

Cultural shadows are thus one of the greatest challenges that multiculturalism faces. Particularly a multiculturalism whose goal is peace and mutual respect between cultures. The very rules of the game have changed.

But changed into what? If I am correct, what are the full implications of these 'shadows'? I don't know. Would that I had the research capabilities and institutional resources to say! The attempt may not even be possible, partly because the subject is so large and wide that it would take a massive amount of research — principally (to heighten the paradox) online research — and research funding and organized efforts to map those implications, and partly because of the speed with which the phenomena change. But some understanding is surely better than none, and a better understanding on the phenomena is surely possible. I can only hope my comments inspire further research.

Few subjects are more amenable to research. If there is one thing that can be said of the internet, it is trackable. Online activity can not only be followed but recorded. The numbers are there, and they can be crunched. We are now theoretically better able to trace the developments and evolution of a culture, online or off, better than ever before.

And if the sheer amount of data is too torrential for us to handle, we now have Artificial Intelligence as well to help us sort the wheat from the chaff. Though the assistance it may provide has some disturbing caveats. Cultural shadows are expressions of a living underlying culture, of living beings. But much of the commentary on the web comes not from living beings, but from bots and AIs. Some are trolls, some are marketing algorithms, some the automated intelligence gathering and propaganda of intelligence agencies.

Certain components of today's cultural shadows are

therefore independent—autonomous. Might cultural shadows themselves become   autonomous at some point? The thought is disturbing.

And yet will these trends go away? No. For better or worse, an inevitable aspect of cultures today is their online expression. And every day that expression is undergoing a dialectical transformation that is transforming the cultures from which they emerge in turn. The tail is wagging the dog, and in so doing it is transforming all our previous cultural verities with it.

In the end, the solutions—and the future—may lie with the psychologists.

B. F. Skinner observed that cultural behavior was shaped by reinforcement, and that the strongest reinforcers are the most immediate. Information itself is a reinforcer, and nothing supplies it faster on in more abundance than the internet. Its capacity to shape cultural behavior—for good or ill—is, from a behavioral perspective, overwhelming. Skinner would no doubt be exceptionally disheartened to see that the reinforcers it now dispenses are so random and accidental and haphazardly applied; but he might also take consolation in his trust in evolution, and the fact that within that frame it is the fittest variations that survive.

Evolutionary psychologists would not be as optimistic. We evolved to be part of a particular kind of society, they say: a physical, tactile, real society in which people interacted face-to-face in small groups for hundreds of millennia. They argue that we are simply not genetically designed to stare at screens eleven hours a day or have strong associations with people we have never actually met or seen o spoken to in real life. The result is that we are all caught up in "a paradoxical form of perception which can be identified as detached involvement," as one commentator on Marshall McLuhan put it, even as McLuhan himself argued that post-literate immersion in the flux of electronic media resulted in a radical dissolution of private identity.

At some level, we all know that the world we see on screen is not entirely real. Nor, increasingly, are we. We have become avatars: our online representations go forth into the internet and speak for us, stand in for us, but they are not us. The resulting alienation from the real leads to a mild schizophrenia, attested to by the skyrocketing growth in depression, anxiety, social anomie, and political terror—the inevitable outcomes of our unalterable mis-adaptation. We cannot resist the internet, yet we are not, in the end, discarnate beings. We are real ones.

"The global village is populated with 'discarnate' human beings who no longer exist as physical presences," wrote Marshall McLuhan. "Instead, the electronic or discarnate person is simply an image or an information pattern, nothing more ... "

But we *are* more. And so, the psychological argument will have to be broadened—in the next chapter.

Chapter Eight

Cultural
Psychotherapy

Cultural Psychotherapy

Readers of the last chapter may be surprised that, in a long piece devoted to something as overt and measurable as internet usage, I chose to conclude with an argument between two different schools of psychology. What does psychology have to do with cultural representations online? Or, for that matter, with world peace? Isn't peace something extrinsic, a matter of treaties and negotiations, an affair of documents and institutional activities that we can see and observe in the outer world? Isn't peace something objective and outward-facing? Why conclude with disciplines that seem principally to look within?

The answer is: because human societies, like human beings, exist as a living whole, and we cannot understand either by only giving our attention to what is without. We also have to explore what is within, the subjectivity of peace, the invisible drivers of our actions, the unconscious drivers of our conscious actions, the impulses of the spirit. In the process of working on behalf of better cultural relations for non-governmental organizations and with UNESCO, and in my academic and private studies, I found a great deal of my work involving representatives of different cultures to be matters of action and activities, but a good deal also involved simply listening, simply attending to cultural sensitivities — simple empathy. I came to see how strongly the subjective shapes the objective, to how deeply the internal accounts for the external.

So, amid all my outer activities, I found myself drifting more and more into reflections and studies about the inner, the psychology of peace, the minds of cultures — the spiritual aspect of cultures and in particular of the culture of peace. I understand that some claim that peace itself is not a culture, or that cultures have no mind of their own at all, that there are only individuals. These positions are not entirely untrue, but they are also splitting hairs.

In actual daily life, different cultures do act in very different ways and interact with very different, very idiosyncratic cultures. We may say that the ways that these different cultures act and interact are ways that are very personality-like. Every collectivity of human beings has an individual profile with its own unique consensus of views, its own internal commonality of attitudes and behaviors. Every culture also has things in common with other cultures. We are, after all, all human, and whatever our histories, humanity shares a common genetic heritage.

Given all this, I found myself wondering if more could be understood about cultures and about peace between cultures if I were to look more closely at "the man behind the curtain," the less apparent drivers behind overt, public cultural characteristics. I found myself thinking about the positive potential of psychological approaches, applied not simply to individual patients, but to cultures and the problems of cultural interactions as a whole.

Now there is nothing new about the idea of a psychology of culture as such. Cultural psychology is an area of academic study all its own. There are many works examining the psychological characteristics of different cultures, and many examining the psychological profiles of individuals within different cultures.

There is even cultural therapy in general, or as some call it, 'culturally sensitive therapy' which emphasizes a therapist's understanding of a client's background, ethnicity, and belief systems. There are areas such as multicultural counseling, in which trained counselors attempt to treat the anxiety or depression of immigrants, refugees and emigres who find it difficult to adjust to their new cultural surroundings. There is an even more focused field, Relational Therapy, sometimes referred to as relational-cultural therapy (RCT), a therapeutic approach basing itself on the notion that "mutually satisfying relationships with others are necessary for one's emotional well- being." Based on the work of Jean Baker Miller, M.D., relational-cultural theory is often aligned with the feminist and or social justice movements in psychology.

Moreover there are entire related fields, such as psychohistory, devoted to examining significant historical figures according to their (presumable) unconscious drives—thousands of pages of speculation devoted to their supposed sexual conflicts and infantile neuroses.

I did not find those later speculations particularly helpful.

Indeed, I did not find much of value in these other fields, but only because I was concerned not with individual psychology or culture in general but with psychology as it might potentially enhance cultures and their peaceful interaction with one another. With therapies not simply for individuals within a culture, but for therapies for cultures as a whole.

These poles are not mutually exclusive. It is undoubtedly a good thing to help a single immigrant, say, adjust to a new and challenging environment. As a new arrival to the United States myself, I could well sympathize! But my main interest was how psychology could advance the cause of world peace, how it could enhance intercultural amity and cooperation. I could find very little in the general schools of psychology as it relates to cultures generally that addressed this macro level.

And yet, among the dross, I found myself striking nuggets of gold. The first such glint that struck me, and drew me forward into years of browsing psychological literature, was the work of psychotherapist Carl Rogers. His approach was amazingly plain: he asserted that the first and primary task of the therapist in the therapeutic situation was simply to listen. Not to change the person, advise the person, improve the person, no. The first task was to create an environment of acceptance, a supportive space for the person to be as they are, to express themselves, to present themselves honestly, without fearing condemnation or criticism or feeling the need to maintain a facade before the gaze of the other.

"Just listen," said Rogers; and in that simplicity I found a priceless and actionable tool.

How often, I reflected, in peace efforts or in our approaches to other cultures, have we projected subtle attitudes of contempt or manipulation? Arriving with its cornucopia of benefits, the First World is forever saying to the nations of the Third World, "Take all these gifts and all this aid, and with our gracious help and charity, perhaps one day you too will be able to rise from your backwardness and become a wonderful First World nation just like us." The condescension of such a one-sided monologue is invisible to such speakers. It never seems to occur to them that other nations might not want to be like them.

What do they want? What do they think they need? How do they see the world? These are often questions that we do not ask at all, or if we do, we ask it in a formal perfunctory manner, as though reading the phrases off a checklist, as a preliminary to the real business of transformation or manipulation—the real business of using the other for our own ends.

From Rogers I learned to ask such questions with genuine sincerity; to provide a space for those of other cultures to present themselves genuinely and comfortably as they are, and to be who they are. Providing a space of total acceptance allowed them to express themselves fully and truthfully. And, as in the person-to-person therapeutic situation, that acceptance resulted in trust—in deeper cultural harmony.

Yes, it was a technique. One simple single technique that I had stumbled across in my random reading. What more could I find as I browsed casually though the entire armory of psychotherapeutic techniques that are unique to what have become hundreds of therapeutic schools? What new tools could I discover?

I discovered more than tools. I found insights. I particularly remember a passage from the great Austrian-born psychoanalyst, Heinz Kohut, as he recounted the depth psychological approach of E. R. Eisler. Wrote Kohut:

> "[Eisler] ... suggested that the history of groups (nations) could be studied as if it were the psychological history of an individual, and he courageously undertook to apply to large groups certain psychological correlations which have proven their explanatory value in the understanding of the individual's mind and of the individual's behavioral propensities. He thus believes that nations can suffer traumata in their early history (parallel to the childhood trauma of the life of an individual). As a consequence of such childhood traumata, repressions can take place, and as a further consequence of such repressions, symptoms, tendencies to irrational acts, to special characterological sensitivities, etc., can develop, just as in the formation of the personality of the individual human being.

> "Ultimately, Eisler expresses his belief that, as the recovery of the repressed through psychoanalytic interpretation enables the individual patient to shed former symptoms and inhibitions and to control former tendencies toward certain rigid reaction patterns, so also with groups and nations."

This passage stunned me. I read it in the context of news items telling me that Palestinian-Israeli peace talks had broken down, and that mutual shelling had resumed. The talks had involved territorial annexation concessions and settlements, and in the light of Eisler's notions I realized that the underlying drivers of the talks were not about detached negotiable matters of property at all, but about the historical sediment of trauma — horrific, deranging trauma.

Is it any wonder that Israelis should want a homeland all their own, a homeland filled with Jewish people, dominated by Jewish people, and held with irrevocable power by Jewish people? Barely a generation ago, these people were literally being hunted down and exterminated — people for whom calls for complete expulsion, even total racial genocide, had echoed down millennia and were still now being made — a genocide that could very well have come about in the lifetime of many Israelis still living. Think of the ardent longing of a homeless person for a home. How much stronger the longing of Jews wandering from nation to nation without a home for over two thousand years!

It was not a matter of agreeing or disagreeing with present-day Israelis about whether settlement borders should be established on this line rather than that one. It was a question of understanding the lasting effects of historical pain, and how it shapes the culture that experiences it, how it continues to cry out silently even in the coolest of present-day heads.

The irony is that in expropriating the homeland of the Palestinians, Israelis transmitted that same suffering, that same pain, to another people, inspiring the very same rage and revulsion towards themselves that had dogged them throughout history. I saw that Israelis and Palestinians facing each other over territorial negotiations were not indifferent brokers, detached and abstract, seeking the best possible real estate arrangements. The diplomats wore masks of calm and might very well have believed in their personal facades of detached rationality. Nonetheless both sides were looking into a mirror, minds conditioned by historical residues of diaspora sorrow, yet blind to the repressed and muted pain and fear in themselves and one another.

What both sides needed was not merely a territorial document—though a just and equitable one for both parties was surely needed as well—but an exploration of their own inner territories.

"Repressions... the tendency to irrational acts, to special characterological sensitivities..." Yes. I could see now how self-evidently these things murmured under diplomatic surfaces, how invisibly yet insistently, and how less than comprehensive and how partial were the best diplomatic methods normally employed. Such methods dismissed rather than addressed the underlying fears and aggressions, and at best created a false temporary pause before a vivid and sometimes violent reappearance. They were matters of the surface, a fragile and transitory repressive surface, through which the repressed material below would inevitably break.

The notion of historical trauma explained so much. The American Civil War ended slavery a century and a half ago. Why then were Americans, black and white, tearing down Civil War statues in public riots? That was like asking, "Why does a traumatized victim return to his trauma in dreams and memories?" Because that is what we do. That is how humans behave. We transform a historical agony into a transhistorical destiny, and live our lives inside the framework of that destiny, that cultural self-definition, that internal picture we hold of one's culture and the culture of the Other, repeatedly playing out our pre-scripted roles, psychologically imprisoned in the dramaturgy of victim and oppressor.

The recent invasion of Ukraine by Russia is another case in point. Have the gains of that invasion justified the costs? The risks? The conflict can't really be explained as a rational geopolitical move. But it makes tremendous sense in the context of Russian paranoia after repeated, devastating, incursions from the West. Having been severely mauled twice, first by Napoleon, next by Hitler, and after decades of nuclear brinksmanship with NATO, Russia could not emotionally tolerate a Ukraine on its border seeking nuclear weapons and discussing NATO membership while similar membership for Russia was denied. Rationally, one might have proposed NATO membership for both Ukraine and Russia, ensuring their mutual security. But how could a European Union, subject to decades of Cold War dread and propaganda, deal rationally enough with its own fears to welcome what it had for so long demonized?

Regarding the victims of "nationalistic narcissistic rage," Kohut writes that, "He regards the offender's mere otherness as an interference with his own omnipotent control over a narcissistically experienced world... The goal remains the total extinction of an enemy, who is experienced as an absolute at each moment in time. No appeal to reason or pity can interfere with this goal, because there is no capacity to be empathic with the enemy, to see a fellow human in him."

No capacity for empathy. No capacity to see the Other, to imagine the Other. Yes—I found myself nodding at that, at the lack of perception and, perhaps above all, the lack of imagination in intercultural relations. Each side was ready to interpret darkly the actions or the other for neither side could imagine the inner world of the other.

Nearly every line in that passage rang true for me. Except for the last line:

> "...as the recovery of the repressed through psychoanalytic interpretation enables the individual patient to shed former symptoms and inhibitions and to control former tendencies toward certain rigid reaction patterns, so also with groups and nations."

There I laughed. Though I suppose I should have wept. Entire nations might well share the same collective response to historical trauma as a single traumatized individual, and that response might indeed mark an entire culture almost indelibly. But was the solution really the 'psychoanalytic interpretation' applied to an individual? Could a whole culture, an entire nation, be expected to lie down on a couch beside a psychoanalyst, discuss its anxieties, and talk about what last night's dream *really* meant?

I shook my head. This was not a practical solution. But—perhaps there was something in psychoanalysis or in related psychologies that pointed to a solution. A way of adapting proven-effective approaches to individuals so that they could at least be somewhat as effective with larger cultural groups. My own understanding of cultures, and the psychic complexity of those cultures and how they dealt with other cultures, had greatly deepened by looking at cultures from this perspective. My very small attempts to adapt therapeutic techniques (such as Rogers') had shown value.

Eisler was wrong: you cannot treat a culture the same way you would an individual. Yet surely there was something about the way a psychotherapist framed and approached the internal problems of a troubled patient that could be adapted and applied to the internal challenges marking a culture. If those challenges could be addressed and healed at such a deeper level, would not a greater harmony between that culture and others follow?

My formal career remained focused on externals: I taught, I lectured, I mentored, I administered, I presented, all to the best of my ability. But once work was done, I found myself diving into the wild seas of psychology and cultural psychology. As I read and studied independently, I would constantly ask myself the question, "How can what we have learned about the mind, how can our collective intelligence, help to ensure peace?" It was my mantra, and I knew that if I repeated it long enough an answer would appear.

The literature of general psychology, even cultural psychology, gave few answers. Why should it? It was about psyche, not history; consciousness, not politics; the historical record of a life, not the utopian possibilities of a culture. The literature of psychotherapy, however, promised positive change, ever-evolving improvement, an increase in sanity and self-understanding—but, overwhelmingly, it was a promise given to the single individual alone, or to small groups. A psychotherapy for entire cultures, much less for the chorus of cultures needed to foster world peace, was missing. There were fragments and glimmers of such a therapy in scholars like Kohl and Eisler, but it was not enough.

I studied on regardless. Perhaps I could find enough fragments of value to one day piece together a whole; or at least to point a direction to other researchers. But there were many disappointments— Freud in particular.

I had decided to explore psychology and its im-plications for cultural harmony in depth, and so I felt I should begin at the foundation of modern psychology. That meant starting with Freud. To my surprise I found reading Freud quite a pleasure, for he was a magnificent writer and he had a flair for writing up his cases in a way that made them read like tales of Sherlock Holmes. The only difference was that instead of a hidden crime, there was a hidden cause of neurosis, and in place of the Master Detective sifting clues and eliminating red herrings till finally unmasking the truth at the end, there was a Master Psychoanalyst doing much the same.

But underneath the pleasure of the narrative, Freud presented a strikingly grim portrayal of humanity. To Freud, humanity was cursed by violent omnidirectional sexual desire that only repression could (barely) contain. Later he tossed aggression as a co-equal partner into the pit where he located the instinctive base roots of the mind. Towards the end of his life he made it a trio by adding a sheer rampaging thirst for savage destruction and self-destruction in the form of a 'Death Instinct.'

The early Freud has seemed something of a liberator, for he had argued that the basis of neurosis and psychosis was sexual repression. The clear implication was that fewer restraints and inhibitions on such behavior would result in more sanity and happiness. It was a popular argument, as you might imagine.

The late Freud was far darker. He continued to state his views that the very embodiments of repression were Civilization and Culture, facades for the reality of repressive control. But now he felt that repression was not a misfortune at all but an iron necessity. The underlying instincts of aggression and death were so strong and anarchic that only severe repression could contain them, and the more severe, he seemed to suggest, the better. Culture was the mind's instrument for crushing the Id, the brute fountain of our destructive and self-destructive drives; and while crushing our instincts via the Ego and Superego would never allow us to be happy, the bloody Saturnalia that would be let loose if those instincts were allowed to run wild was, in his view, worth the price.

Thus, in the Freudian scheme, repression was good, culture was equivalent to repression, and the more repression, the better and more stable social life would be. "Where Id was, there Ego shall be," he prophesied, suggesting that one part of the mind should eradicate the other—a genocide of subjectivity. It is hard not to find in such sentiments a justification for rigid social control; almost a celebration of undisguised fascism.

I simply could not follow Freud there. My strongest objection to it was not intellectual. My strongest objection was my childhood. I did not feel especially repressed as a child, nor were my parents or our neighbors in the Jamaica I knew as a boy agents of cultural tyranny. They seemed rather happy and easy-going to me! To suggest that Jamaican culture was some sort of psychic device intended to stamp the vicious lust and burning suicidal violence in our hearts into dog-like submission was just silly. It simply wasn't an accurate description.

Yet in other respects, what tools there were to be found in Freud! Concepts such as sublimation, via which aggressive and destructive impulses could be muted, channeled, and transfigured into the production of art and music. Could aesthetics be an unexpected road, I wondered, for reducing aggression and fostering cultural harmony?

Or the concept of projection, in which the criticism directed at others is really a revelation of one's own goals and desires? If loathing of the Other provided and image of the Self, could that provide valuable insights into cultures? Certainly.

Or fetishism, the displacement of one's wishes and fantasies onto alternative objects. Wrote Freud, the fetishist is able at one and the same time to believe in his fantasy and to realize that it is nothing but a fantasy, Even recognizing the fantasy as fantasy in no way reduces its power over the individual. How like so many self-deluded political leaders and ideologues, half-believing in their doublethink, half-terrified at the revenge of reality, and yet following their course willfully down to oblivion.

As I read further, I began to realize that just as there was a gulf between psychology as such and psychotherapy, there was an even deeper gulf between cultural psychology and 'cultural psychotherapy.' Psychology has a clear meaning: it is a study of the mind. Psychotherapy has a clear meaning too: it is the study of using our understanding of the mind to help others in mental and emotional distress. There was even a clear meaning to Cultural Psychology: it is the study of the mental worlds of different cultures.

But a science of using our understanding of the mental lives of cultures to help develop those cultures mentally and emotionally, to alleviate states of cultural distress, cultural trauma, cultural neurosis in those cultures? It seemed a logical enough progression, and there were hints in various cultural and psychological articles, but as a formal area it really did not exist.

Yet, as Eisler rightly intuited, it ought to exist. If certain psychotherapeutic approaches could help individuals, if small group therapy was a reality, there is no reason *per se* why such approaches not be utilized to help groups — indeed, to help entire cultures, to allow dysfunctional cultures to recover their cultural sanity, as it were.

'Cultural sanity' — the phrase gave me pause. For how could cultures like that of Nazi Germany, or the totalitarian world of high Stalinism, for instance, be better described than as ill? As cultures out of touch with reality? (And might not cultural shadows be described that way? As cultural worlds out of touch with the reality-grounded cultures that generated them?)

The literature of cultural psychology gave many descriptions of the mental lives of people in different cultures, and much insight into those adjusting to life in another culture. But they provided very little in the way of describing what mental health might be for a culture as a whole. And almost nothing when it came to the question of how a culture might pass from a crippled state to an optimal one, or what techniques could be effectively applied.

Psychotherapy provided many such techniques—for individuals. Why were there not, as yet, psychotherapies for entire cultures? There was no obvious reason. Wasn't it possible to take techniques from psychotherapies proven to have positive results for individuals, and adapt and apply those to those larger collections of individuals we call a culture?

That is what I began doing—intermittently and haphazardly, alas. For as soon as I had the idea, I realized that, as with my notion of 'cultural shadows,' it was an idea that would take an army of researchers and cataracts of funding, neither of which were at my disposal. There were dozens—hundreds—of schools of psychotherapy. There was a vast array of therapeutic interventions. How many could be fruitfully applied to cultures as a whole? Perhaps hundreds! True, some might be dispensed with—there was hardly much point to suggesting that an enraged Palestine take an antidepressant.

But how much of a work like Reich's *Mass Psychology of Fascism* was applicable today? How much of its prescriptions remained valid—if any? How many of them could be revised and updated and used effectively to prevent a new resurgences of fascism in present-day conditions? These were questions that could engage a single scholar for years. To do the same for the full range of existing psychotherapies and distill effective cultural psychotherapies would be a titanic endeavor requiring lifetimes.

That said, there are titanic endeavors that are well worth the undertaking; and if even one of the approaches discovered along the way was enough to minimize or deflect the darkness of an emerging war or possible genocide, surely the effort would be worth it. I did not have the arrogance to imagine that I could create the full and final psychotherapeutic solution for all future cultural issues, but I felt I could select a few promising techniques from among the hundreds available and possible adapt some of those. And if I could not do it all myself, perhaps I could inspire others. So, as always, I kept studying and accumulating more notes. It would be a long road, possibly stretching beyond my lifetime, but I felt that my journey 'towards cultural intelligence' had well and truly begun.

I was especially heartened by the developing evolution of the therapeutic field. What we now call psychotherapy had begun with Freud, but, mercifully, it had not stopped there. This is by no means to dismiss or disrespect Sigmund Freud's great contributions. The simple fact, however, was that, over time and after enough empirical examination, it became apparent that Freudian psychotherapy was rarely very successful. Freud himself suggested as much in one of his later essays, "Analysis Terminable And Interminable." Even the Master began to notice that some of his patients had been going to therapy for decades and were not much improved.

Further studies by statisticians confirmed that observation, adding that not a few such patients were worse off after their 'psychoanalytic interpretation' than before. Freud the thinker had made many astute observations about the mind, but Freud the doctor and Freudian analysis had very few successes,

That realization was progress—genuine progress. The search for more effective variations followed, and soon other psychologists tried getting it right, beginning with the Freudians themselves. Freudian heretics—Jung, Reich, Adler, and many more—soon began founding their own schools and developing novel alternative approaches. Some were genuine improvements, others not, but nearly all had something of value to contribute.

Just as technology improves from the joint effort of many minds seeking to optimize its operations, and just as experiment shows that some optimizations work better than others, soon stronger and more effective psychotherapies began to develop—in particular, one that had a great impact on my thinking.

This was the behavior therapy that developed from the work of B. F. Skinner. Although I should honestly say that Skinner the man personally had quite as much an impact.

I was dazzled by the writings of B. F. Skinner. I was also repelled by them. It must be said that no one till Skinner had put psychology on more of a scientific basis. It must also be said that no one worked harder to erase all humanity from human psychology.

Skinner had no professional interest at all in the substance of subjectivity—in thoughts, feelings, love, hate, desire, rage, aggression, religious ecstasy, moral fervor, inward reflection. He redefined all psychology as the study of measurable behavior, and of the environmental conditions that influenced measurable behavior. 'Man' was not his subject at all, nor was

'Mind'—the only things that concerned him were the precise conditions under which 'the organism,' as he referred to experimental subjects from mouse to man, behaved.

Unsurprisingly, he began his studies with mice, and pigeons, and examined how making small changes to the consequences of their actions affected their actions. He soon found that making certain changes completely controlled their behavior.

These changes largely revolved around his concept of reinforcement, which is often assumed to be equivalent to the concept of reward. It is not. Suffice it to say, if 'an organism' experienced a consequence immediately after emitting a behavior, that demonstrably resulted in the behavior becoming more likely to occur once again. If so, that consequence was said to reinforce the behavior. Pleasure, obviously was a very good reinforcer, though different subjects might find different things pleasurably, hence reinforcing. If there was no consequence following a behavior, or a punishing consequence following a behavior, less of the behavior would follow.

On this amazingly slender base, Skinner constructed an adequate explanation for all human and mammalian behavior, and a methodology for behavior modification that is still stronger than any challenger, then or now. His approaches worked, and worked consistently.

Here, if anywhere, was where lasting and universal peace on earth could be engineered, I thought. Here was how enduring harmony between all human cultures could be built. Here was where the final answer was to be found! Or so I thought.

Needless to say, that first rich blush of enthusiasm

has since moderated somewhat, though I still consider behaviorism to be the leading contender for the study of effective cultural transformation. The misfortune was that Skinner conflated the science of behaviorism and his philosophy of behaviorism, and they are two very different things. The philosophy proved so unpalatable and repugnant that the implicit social science, tragically, has been largely shunned to this day.

The problem was, Skinner believed that genetics plus environment totally determined all human actions and all human thoughts. For Skinner, freedom did not exist anywhere for anyone or anything. Soul, spirit, subjectivity were complete, utter and irrelevant illusions. The world as he saw it was utterly devoid of God, morality, choice, personal decision, or responsibility. In Skinner's view, we all have the misfortune to be robots in a robotic universe who only imagine that our thoughts are somehow independent of the brains that generate them automatically without our participation. Give up the illusion of freedom, the illusion that you are really a person, said Skinner, and let a system of behavioral conditioning control you and improve your personal condition. Why? He had no ultimate answer. Why not?

Who would control and operate such a system? The system itself would condition rulers to operate in the interests of the system. It would be a rule of Enlightened Despotism without a Despot.

Skinner's philosophical interpretation of his science was so off-putting that, though Skinner's successes at behavior modification were greater than any such attempts ever seen before, Skinner's leadership position in American psychology was soon overthrown.

Behaviorism was replaced by Cognitive Science, which was a study of Mind, the entity Skinner simply rejected out of hand. Cognitive Science is not therapy and has not proved remotely as successful as Skinner's operant conditioning when it comes to modifying human behavior.

But it was a lot more reinforcing.

The story did not stop there. From that division, Cognitive-Behavior Therapy (CBT) emerged, which posited that modifying behaviors and thoughts was the most effective way to foster therapeutic change.

Numerous patient result studies suggest that CBT is the most widely effective therapy in operation today. Numerous other flavors of cognitive- behavior therapy have also emerged — Rational-Emotive Behavior Therapy (REBT), Dialectical Behavior Therapy (DBT), Functional Analytic Psychotherapy (FAP), Behavioral Activation (BA), Virtual Reality Therapy (VRT) Brief Therapy, etc. (All this, alongside numerous non-behavioral therapies of every stripe, from Jungian Therapy to Adlerian Therapy to Gestalt Therapy to ever- persistent classical Freudian analysis.)

None of these are specifically geared to the question of how best to engage cultures to co-exist in peace with one another, however; and the labor of analyzing the techniques of each school with an eye to weighing and adapting the most promising of such techniques to that goal is, as I have said, a massive project requiring a vast consortium on scholars.

There was one major psychologist, however, who made a notable effort to create an explicit methodology of cultural design. Surprisingly, that too was B. F. Skinner.

It may be wondered why Skinner, who did not regard people as people (as we understand the term), should have given so much time and thought to creating a genuinely peaceful and enduring utopian culture for everyone. But he did. He would attribute it to his history and environment, but I prefer to ascribe it to an inner humanity in the man that he scrupulously denied. By all accounts he was personally as kind and decent a person as one could be, with a streak of social benevolence that is jarringly at odds with his overall philosophy.

Whatever his reasons, he wrote a number of papers in the latter part of his life that were explicitly utopian, and which described how his highly effective behavioral techniques could be used to bring them about.

Sadly, he did not leave behind a full set of detailed blueprints. But in his characteristically titled book, *Beyond Freedom And Dignity,* he wrote two major chapters, *The Evolution Of A Culture*, and *The Design Of A Culture*, that make strong arguments that existing cultures are already designed by (usually unknown and random) consequences, and that the conscious design of radically improved human cultures are achievable.

Are these just theory? No. In his novel, *Walden Two,* Skinner presented a portrait of a real-life behavioral community in operation. Small, modest, self-sufficient and peaceful, it is perhaps the greatest addition to utopian literature of our era. More to the point, it inspired and continued to inspire actual communities based on its principles, from Twin Oaks to Los Horcones to several others. These communities do in fact function. They are actual, real, and peaceful, communities. If more than one successful experiment can be taken as a confirmation of the theory behind it. Skinner has confirmed the viability of a communitarian realization of his ideas.

With one major caveat. No one has ever managed to apply those ideas to mass society or to existing mass cultures. The world of Walden Two, and the actual communities based on it, are communities of dozens or at most hundreds of people. Extrapolating from that small scale to non-behavioral actually existing communities of millions and hundreds of millions in a world of nearly eight billion people and rising is another matter.

Skinner, of course, would disagree. He would argue that every society is as completely subject to the laws of behavior as any other. The only difference, he would point out, is that world society today has been designed accidentally and disastrously.

But even on the macro scale his approach has some empirical support.

The appearance of Philip Kotler's and Nancy R. Lee's *Social Marketing: Influencing Behaviors For Good*, while not explicitly Skinnerian, incorporates several implicit behavioral models in a ground-breaking attempt to market socially responsible behavior. The classic case— and a successful one—involves the use of advertising and marketing media to reduce cigarette smoking.

One of the core principles of behaviorism is that where a behavior-consequence relationship is modeled by others, or established by repeated statements ('rules'), it has the same effect, weaker but nonetheless real, as an real-life behavior followed by a directly experienced consequence. Presentation alone, therefore (via advertisements and TV commercials and other marketing media), is predicted to have a degree of the same effectiveness, and practice has confirmed this. Where the campaigns have been applied, they have worked. They have not worked perfectly—smoking has not been universally eradicated. But it has been significantly reduced. Schools calling themselves social behaviorists have noted these attempts and created statistical models of effectiveness. Applied to large populations, the interventions have measurable impacts.

If social marketing campaigns can reduce cigarette smoking, can similar campaigns reduce violence? Can they foster peace and cultural harmony? We can say with some certainty that they can—to a degree. How can we ensure that that degree rises in scope and penetration and effectiveness? What other techniques are waiting to be discovered or created? Time will tell.

The original Walden was one man seeking peace of mind by living in isolation, distant from others beside wooded pond. Walden Two was a fictional community of a thousand people living in peace, leading to several real communities in which people have been living in peace for decades.

What will the next Walden be—an online community of tens of thousands, a 'cultural shadow' of millions, perhaps? Of billions?

I spoke in the last chapter about my concerns involving these digital 'cultural shadows,' but perhaps not enough about their potential. Major corporate social media are making considerable efforts these days to minimize hate speech and terrorist activities on their platforms; China and Russia, with their somewhat heavy-handed attempts to forge and manage national internets, are nonetheless attempting to use it to shape their cultures.

It is not too much to hope that in coming days they will use their digital   domains not merely to foster support for their existing regimes, but to shape their cultures in other, more beneficial, ways.

The larger point, however, is that, yes, there are tools with which peace can be built, tools that have been tested in practice with individuals, with small groups, and which have been shown to have influenced large ones. The techniques and technologies are there, and many of the most effective are to be found in the world of psychotherapy, where approaches to human betterment has been studied for over a century and where many of those approaches and techniques have been successfully applied to millions—though not, as yet, to entire cultures as a whole.

But the techniques are there in embryo, waiting to be unearthed and developed and applied. And based on the record so far, they work.

It is the task of cultural intelligence to discover and further hone and apply such tools. We are fortunate that the foundations of that task have already been built.

Chapter Nine

Existential Multiculturalism

Existential Multiculturalism

Journalists these days seem to have fallen in love with the word 'existential.' Every crisis is an 'existential crisis,' every threat an 'existential threat.' They apparently regard the term as being synonymous with 'Very Important!' and use it to add further drama to whatever new item they are currently sensationalizing.

But using the term as seasoning to sell newspapers has nothing to do with its actual meaning, which derives from the nineteenth-century century Danish philosopher and Christian, Søren Kierkegaard, the father of modern existential philosophy.

Kierkegaard considered that what gave meaning to each individual's life was the lived experience of the individual: his or her existence—not ideology, not government, not Church or Mosque or Synagogue, not their social role or the parts others expected them to play, not the mob. Each individual had the fundamental challenge of living sincerely, truthfully, "authentically."

To Kierkegaard, subjective human experience mattered quite as much or more than the supposedly objective truths of science or research. To assume a supposedly detached, observational, outside perspective was, to Kierkegaard, a form of self-deception. That sort of approach might well uncover extrinsic facts of some importance, and that was good. But not if it overlooked and stifled deeper and more profound inner truths.

Existentialists sought not simply to accumulate facts, but to face the deeper reality of their own human experience, to overcome the distractions and diversions and meaningless bustle of modern life, to freely examine and define and shape the nature of their own existence.

Kierkegaard went so far as to argue that that the objective certainty of any number of so-called facts was ultimately impossible to gauge, but that through a "Leap of Faith," human beings could transcend the limitations of their situation and rise to a higher inner stage of existence, one that gave meaning and ethical value to their life.

Could the truth of Christianity (or Islam, or Buddhism) be demonstrated in the same way that the existence of the atom could be demonstrated, or the fact that the Earth revolves around the Sun? No, he admitted. But such truths could be *embraced*; and that decisive embrace, that leap, could transfigure people, transform them and give their lives as a whole new purpose, meaning and order.

In this way, such a person, one whom Kierkegaard called the "Knight of Faith," could transcend and put aside the nihilism of the modern world, and by their free choice gracefully actualize their human fullness. "The knight of faith is the only happy man, the heir to the finite," said Kierkegaard in Either/Or, because while the knight of faith might not have certainty as to outer material facts, he had inner certainty as to his own integrity, his own freely chosen selfhood.

What, you may ask, has any of this to do with multiculturalism?

Simply that one of the core themes running through his book has been peaceful cultural coexistence is a lived experience, a felt reality. So many books and articles and trainings present multiculturalism as a sociological datum, an indifferent fact of modern life that one must accept and deal with efficiently in order to maximize office efficiency or enhance social lubrication.

That is not enough. It is not even 'real' in the sense of being true to our experience. It is like the abstraction 'peace' used as a synonym for the mere absence of war. We cannot embrace something that is not. We can only embrace something which is. And we cannot truly embrace even that, unless what 'is' is vivid, compelling, attractive.

I have talked about the multiculturalism of my childhood, where difference was not a disturbance but a continual surprise and delight. I have also discussed multiculturalism as an academic subject to which I have devoted many years of study.

But consider the contrast between my experiences as a child as opposed to the massive amount of reading and study about multiculturalism I underwent as I was writing my dissertation on cultural competence.

As a child and young man, I casually met people from all sorts of backgrounds who differed in all sorts of ways. We chatted, ate together, waved to one another in the street, joked, told stories. I lived with them and among them. I liked them.

In the course of writing my dissertation, I encountered a great many words in a great many books and met a few people in the course of contexts such as an academic interview.

The experiences were not the same.

Now there is certainly nothing wrong with gathering all the detailed data one can on society and social interactions. Indeed, the findings of more scholarly and objective research concerning multiculturalism are completely compatible with existential multiculturalism, just as an objective medical or behavioral report on a subject is entirely compatible with the fact that the person under study possesses subjectivity. That subjectivity is an added dimension, but not only an added dimension. It can be the key element in that subject's health and behavior.

Objective analysis retains all its rights and value. However, I would argue that there is a profound gulf between such detached social analysis and living interaction, between a detached analysis of differences and the will to live peaceably among others and embrace their differences.

This is the gap we must fill. It calls for the practice of an existential multiculturalism, where the emphasis is on choosing, not suffering, the experience of the new; on experiencing multiculturalism with emotional openness and full personal authenticity, rather than with merely formal tolerance. It is not a multiculturalism of default. What we must cultivate is a multiculturalism of feeling; more than that, a multiculturalism of enjoyment and pleasure. The modern world with its ease of travel, its need of labor, its immigration and refugee policies, its borderless news, and social media, make multiculturalism an unavoidable feature of personal and public life. This is not a misfortune we have to endure with reluctance. It can be at the very least an endless series of refreshing novelties, and at the best a blessing, an opportunity for learning and personal growth which we can learn to encounter with appreciation and joy.

So urgent is this modern need in a world still stricken with conflict and tempted by terror and violence that I am tempted to quote W. H. Auden's striking line from his poem, September 1, 1939, "We must love one another or die."

Except for the fact that the line is quite wrong: we must love one another in order to truly live.

If this seems like high rhetoric, I assure you it is not. One could fill entire libraries with anecdotes of positive experiences and interactions between persons of one culture and another. Books and memoirs abound full of such stories. Drama and the arts abound in them. Not only culture but pop culture is filled with the joys of the unfamiliar, from Doctor Who to *The King and I* to *E.T.* We have as much a thirst for the new and different as we do for the known and the comfortable. It is only a matter of how the new is first presented to us, whether in a positive or in a negative manner.

But when multiculturalism is understood by us and an imposition, the presence of a faceless 'them' that is empty of positive content, it is all too easy to fill it with images of apprehension and fear. When it is an actual human being that we see, an actual face looking back at our own, that apprehension begins to dissolve. The unknown becomes known, the strange familiar, the unexpected comforting.

As with multiculturalism, so with peace. To most people, peace is bland and featureless. War, by contrast, is all too rich in emotional content. It comes fully packaged with patriotism and love of country. It calls on our bravery, our commitment to defend home and hearth, our solidarity with our fellows. Planes fly, troops march, bombs explode. War is exciting. Is it any wonder that nations and peoples slip into it so naturally?

We will never cast off our self-destructive love of war or develop a greater love for peace unless we manage to redefine peace as having some stronger and more attractive substance, as a state that stirs the emotions even higher than the high dramas of conflict, that lifts hearts and inspires vision.

This is why I have repeatedly brought up the subject of utopia. It is utopia that is the proper content of peace—that presents an idealized world that addresses our deepest longings and promises to satisfy them.

The longer I have thought about what it means to strive for and achieve peace, the more utopia has assumed a larger and larger place in my mind.

Though I've browsed psychologies of all sorts, preferring to be the jack of all trades to being the master of one, I've dwelt in this book largely on one psychologist, B. F. Skinner, because what appeals to me about his work is not so much his metaphysics or even his method as the fact that he was a conscious architect of cultures—a conscious architect of utopia.

That may sound strange coming from a student of culture. After all, utopia literally means 'no place'—it is a culture that does not exist, and that therefore can never be studied at all!

But what is the notion of world peace, of the peaceful unity of all humankind, if not utopian? Peace and cultural harmony are not mirages, not delusions—they are genuine objects of study. For we have experienced periods of peace, we have witnessed times of mutual support and alliance between different nations and cultures. History fluctuates, and such moments may come and go. But they have existed, and so the conditions of their existence as well as the conditions of their coming and their going can be realistically examined.

Spaces of peace exist, and have always existed. But the enduring global peace of which I dream has never existed. And so, one must more than dream it. One must plan. One has to envision a goal in order to strive for it. One has to imagine an outcome make it real. To imagine it in enough detail and with enough charisma and grace to make it compelling.

Why does Utopia matter to peace? Not because it's achievable, though I believe that satisfying enough approximations are achievable, but because it's desirable. We long for a better world; we long for better lives; we ache for release from our struggles, for freedom from our fears, for an escape from our limitations. Thus, we are motivated to seek that release, that escape, that freedom. We are fortunate to have such motivation, for if we could not develop a love for peace, we will never achieve it.

An existential multiculturalism calls us to such heights by calling us to attend to our inner depths. By mindful self-examination focusing on the inward aspects of cultural openness and acceptance, we lift ourselves above the laziness of fear, the sloth of automatic aversion. By actively seeking out the value in the Other, by imaginatively experiencing the gifts of our potential symbioses, we pave the way for a multiculturalism of enjoyment, of mutual reinforcement. We continually focus on the problems of multiculturalism and how to resolve them. Such efforts are well worth making, but we should cultivate too a focus on the joys of multiculturalism, on the possibility of multicultural utopia.

I believe we all have an inner understanding that such a multicultural utopia is possible. What is Star Trek if not a popular intuition of that possibility, or the many Utopias from Sir Thomas More to Callenbach's Ecotopia if not records of our longings for that possibility, and its precursors?

Yet all these idealistic locales never address the place where they can truly be found: within.

It is in this regard that I must mention the great East German philosopher of Utopia, Ernst Bloch.

The whole of Ernst Bloch's thick philosophical oeuvre stems from Marx's remark that religion is a vision of the perfected world that Marxism seeks to materially construct. To Bloch, oppression was the speck of dust from which the pearl of Utopia takes its start. Marx might have considered religion to be merely the 'sigh of the oppressed creature,' but Bloch realized that implicit in all oppression was a heartfelt cry for its reversal, for the implicit Utopia hidden within that suffering. As the American mystic Neville Goddard wrote, "If you were in debt, freedom from debt would be the solution. If you were hungry, food would be the solution... The sick man's savior is health, the hungry man's savior is food, the thirsty man's savior is water." Just so: it is the lost who most fervently crave salvation, the empty who most passionately crave fulfillment. Far from being 'unworldly,' said Bloch, religion provides humanity the social blueprints of the future. Out of the depths it brings a vision of those depths transcended.

As Bloch wrote:

> "It is a question of learning hope. Its work does not renounce, it is in love with success rather than failure. Hope, superior to fear, is neither passive like the latter, nor locked into nothingness. The emotion of hope goes out of itself, makes people broad instead of confining them, cannot know nearly enough of what it is that makes them inwardly aimed, of what may be allied to them outwardly.
>
> "The work of this emotion requires people who throw themselves actively into what is becoming, to which they themselves belong... it looks in the world itself for what can help the world... How richly people have always dreamed of this, dreamed of the better life that might be possible.
>
> "Nobody has ever lived without day-dreams, but it is a question of knowing them deeper and deeper and in this way keeping them trained unerringly, usefully, on what is right. Let the daydreams grow

even fuller, since this means they are enriching themselves around the sober glance; not in the sense of clogging, but of becoming clear. Not in the sense of merely contemplative reason which takes things as they are and as they stand, but of participating reason which takes them as they go, and therefore also as they could go better. Then let the daydreams grow really fuller, that is, clearer, less random, more familiar, more clearly understood and more mediated with the course of things. So that the wheat which is trying to ripen can be encouraged to grow and be harvested."

It is rather in this sense that I see an existential multiculturalism arising and becoming an inevitability. We do not want to be aliens in an alien landscape. We do not want to be "a stranger and afraid / In a world I never made." We do not have to be, if we make the existential choice to be something better. We want to love. We want to be accepted, respected, cherished. We dream of peace. A truly existential multiculturalism chooses the multicultural world that is our heritage, accepts it with deliberate joy, acknowledges its challenges and surprises with vital enthusiasm.

Do not imagine that I am saying that we need to push ourselves into becoming emotional and enthusiastic about living in a multicultural world. It is not a matter of getting worked up, of forcing oneself to feel positive about the regular presence of other cultures.

True, existentialism clearly and explicitly emphasizes subjectivity and lived personal experience. An existential perspective is never cold and detached, and never stands outside the direct involvement that is an ineradicable part of human life. It denies that such detachment is even possible for the individual human being and decries all such attempts as inauthentic.

But it would be no less of a mistake to dismiss existentialism as purely irrational or emotional. Serious personal commitment does not dismiss intellectual acuity: it demands it. Existentialism is a philosophy of feeling, but not only of feeling, and it is the presence and delicate balance between both aspects of existentialism that make it so valuable for a living experience of cultural diversity. For existentialism is also a body of thought, a framework of understanding. Like the wide range of contemporary psychotherapies, it is composed of dozens, arguably hundreds, of distinct and individual schools, and, again like the psychotherapies, each school can cast a unique and illuminating light upon the multicultural.

To give only two examples:

Consider merely the possibility of a *Heideggerian multiculturalism*. The great German philosopher was famous for his description of time and history as intrinsic components of *Dasein*—of individual human experience. So often we think of multiculturalism as a kind of association between fixed social entities—that Palestinians are like this, and Israelis are like that, or that Russians behave this way, Ukrainians that way, and cultural relations between such groups must always therefore be a collision, a battle between communities frozen in time. From a Heideggerian perspective, however, the present moment is composed of people who have a felt relationship to differently interpreted pasts and equally personal anticipations of different futures. They are changing individuals embedded in an equally fluctuating understandings of themselves and their cultures and their relations to other cultures.

Far from being fixed and frozen, a Heideggerian perspective evokes both primordial heritages and evolving possibilities—a multiculturalism in which the cultures more closely resemble time than space. Is that a novel, liberating perspective? Does it give us new ways of thinking through our situation, of formulating new and unique solutions? Obviously.

Or consider Sartre. For all his intellectual debts to Heidegger, the French philosopher is strikingly different from the German. Sartre took an explicitly atheist stance; he not only did not believe in God, but he did also not quite believe in humankind either, whom he described as "a hole in Being." His psychoanalytic writings concerning the unconscious argued that human beings had no unconscious: that people were defined by the conscious mind and *only* the conscious mind. Ultimately, in his *Critique of Dialectical Reason*, his views mutated into a sort of post-existentialist Maoism.

But some of Sartre's views are priceless for students of multiculturalism. No one argued more forcefully for total human freedom. We are the sum of our conscious choices, argued Sartre, we are completely free to become whatever we want to be. Sartre did not write very much about multiculturalism specifically, but he would surely argue that multiculturalism is an existential choice: that how we relate to our cultures and other cultures is a *decision*, that we *construct* our cultural selves and *consciously fashion* our actions, and the way we react and interact with others and other cultures. Again, does such an existential framework allow us to conceive the reality of our multicultural experiences in new and possibly more valuable ways? Of course.

There are existentialisms of the mind as well as the heart; call them existentialisms of the spirit. Neither they nor more secular existentialisms present us with fixed dogmas intended to limit thought, but rather additional tools with which to probe our modern multicultural environment and our personal reactions to it, and each school allows us to do so in rich new ways. Personally, I find that the religious existentialists—figures like Tillich, J. J. Altizer, Neibuhr, Barth, Berdyaev—have at least as much contribute, addressing as they do the ontological fatigue of a world increasingly absorbed into the shifting play of its cultural shadows.

But the more practical takeaway for those working for peace and cultural harmony is that viewing our multicultural reality through such existential lenses allow us to see that reality—and our responses and responsibilities to it—in wider and more thoughtful senses. Such a freshly expanded understanding is not only emotional, and not only a matter of heightened commitment, although it embraces and enhances such personal options, choices that are valuable too. Rather it is a path leading to living and understanding our world and ourselves in greater depth. Can that help lead to peace? Even if it leads only to greater inner peace, it is a journey worth taking.

The isolationism of ethno-nationalists is no longer

an option in a digitally connected world where every nation's well-being is depended upon a global supply chain to which all contribute. We have become globally interdependent. Our individual survival and the quality of our individual lives is tied up with the survival and quality of life of others with very different views and lifestyles. That is simply a fact. How do we deal with it? Will we adopt a personally supportive or a personally destructive standpoint in regards to that fact?

The reality of our global interdependence does not mean that we are imprisoned, or that our local way of life needs to cast aside. Multiculturalism values all cultures, equally supporting one's own. It means that we have the option of seeing ourselves as members of a global community in which differences are not the mark of a stranger, but something common and universal.

How then can we live life well in a multicultural world?

I propose that best answer is an existential multiculturalism—not a reluctant multiculturalism which imprisons ourselves and others under racial or ethnic or ideological labels, but one that celebrates the unique interiority one's culture confers upon the individual, but that also accepts and embraces our passage through a continuing landscape of novelty and change—a landscape that is now our universal culture.

A science fiction writer once said that the future is a foreign country into which we are all being deported. Why not rather a foreign country which we are eager to tour? For we are all travelers now, and every passing few months is an arrival in a new world. Like the philosopher Heraclitus, we cannot step into the same river twice: the flow of time is too strong and moves too swiftly. But we can sail that river gracefully, with competence and skill, alert to the changes in the sea and the wind, aided by our shipmates who have gathered from many lands.

It is a novel sort of existence, for humanity has a long tribal history of remaining in place among close kin. But it is the way we live now, and it is a world which we can navigate skillfully and well; for no culture is alien: all cultures are branches of our one common root, universal humanity, and in the end the Other is ourself.

Chapter Ten

Toward Cultural Intelligence

Toward
Cultural Intelligence

I have called this book *Toward Cultural Intelligence,* not *About* Cultural Intelligence. I did so to explicitly signal that I am approaching new phenomena, new areas of research and study, rather than reporting about areas already exhaustively explored in detail. I also believe that these new areas are related, and so I have brought them together under the term, 'Cultural Intelligence.'

But I want to clarify what this collection of areas, Cultural Intelligence, is not. Cultural Intelligence is not a rejection of my own work in Cultural Competence, much less a rejection of the titanic scholarship of many decades of cultural studies in a vast range of fields.

I have spoken of the phenomenon I call Existential Multiculturalism, a way and a will to experience our new global multicultural social reality via an inwardness, a spiritual movement of the whole person, one which grounds us and prompts us to action and commitment. Neither should that in any way be taken as a rejection of Cultural Competence. Results gathered in that field retain their validity and their full value. I now believe that those studies did not express the full existential dimension of the multicultural experience, but in going beyond that earlier perspective I am not casting it aside; rather, I'm seeking to explore a further dimension to it, to widen and deepen and heighten what remains valuable in such earlier work.

Cultural Competence; Existential Multiculturalism. These two are not opposites, but rather poles of the same single phenomenon. Cultural Intelligence adds a still further dimension that embraces and extends both, in a combination that for that reason is different from and greater than both. Just as human beings are a mixture of reason and emotion, so Cultural Intelligence is a harmonious bringing together of exteriority and interiority, of dissecting intellect and driving emotion. To bring about global peace, not only is a harmony between extrinsic cultures needed, but also a harmony within, a harmony of mind and soul, of outer action and inner reflection. What I call Cultural Intelligence preserves the scholarly scientific intellectual quest for social truth while at the same time fostering the emotional and spiritual drivers that must be cultivated if world peace is ever to be achieved.

From childhood to today I have tried to encounter culture and cultural harmony at this deep level, the level of direct personal experience. It humbles me to reflect that I could encounter it so much more easily as a child, when other cultures and people of those cultures so comfortably accepted it as a simple and delightful part of life. Since then, I have tried to understand culture and cultural interaction intellectually. That attempt has borne valuable but complex fruit, for time and again I would come up against the surprise of the real.

I visited Guyana and Suriname expecting island cultures much like Jamaica and found spaces as different from Jamaica as from each other. I went to Cuba half-expecting a grey Communist Gulag and found a pleasant easy-going population enjoying their long lunches in a virtual museum of astonishing European architecture. In Switzerland I expected cuckoo clocks and instead stumbled upon a living moment of Utopia. In America I expected the moral simplicity and lawless freedom of a John Wayne movie, and instead I found a complexity of sub-cultures and a Dada-like collage of shifting contradictory norms.

In the best-funded educational systems on the face of the earth I found students obsessed principally with attire and physical appearance. In the service of charitable institutions, I found the supreme focus lay on fund-getting. At the United Nations, where every scheduled speech received an international public spotlight, I found the most profound and effective moments took place in quiet, unplanned private conversations over coffee and tea. In every case, the reality of what I experienced subtly escaped the expectations with which I approached it.

The extrinsic knowledge that the world of scholarship has gathered about cultures, coupled with training in scientific methodologies that yielded them, has produced many insights based on that close detailed cultural analysis. Those insights helped inform my understanding and appreciations tremendously. Indeed, a good deal of my life has been given over to joining in efforts and contributing to such knowledge. In my dissertation I sought to better define cultural competence and to demonstrate that certain forms of training and instruction could expand such competence into more areas.

Armed with such valuable research information led me to further contemplate multiculturalism and how best to navigate it. But they are not only abstract objects of study. They are lived experiences; they are things we experience with the entirety of ourselves, with what Germans call our *Geist*—mind, soul, intellect, spirit, intermingled in wholeness and unity. Cultural Intelligence is my term for that wholeness, an approach and response to our multicultural environment involving intellect and feeling, objectivity and subjectivity, a unification of the whole person mindfully encountering the living communities of others, and mindfully, as though for the first time, striving to truly see the community in which they themselves live.

Such cultural intelligence speaks of an intense, a personal, almost ontological moment when one approaches the Other from an inner standpoint, a communion I call existential because it is not solely an exercise of competence but a communion of being. I call that moment the presence and exercise of 'cultural intelligence': not an action that one does, or a role that one plays, but a moment when one is.

This state of being does not transcend the world as we know and experience it. It does not dispense with thought and reflections and intellect. On the contrary: it aims to connect with the world more closely on that level, as well as on all levels.

Earlier in this book I described a phenomenon I have come to call the 'cultural shadow,' an appropriation and absorption of human cultural interaction into the internet, where we now wander and gasp much like the first amphibians clambering onto the new mediums of air and shore.

After poring over innumerable journal articles in university library stacks, I came not to merely gather facts about it but to reflect on it as it touched on my own direct day-to-day experience. By pulling together what was known and studied, both public analyses and private psychology, and what were personally encountered, I began to see the wisdom, not (only) of psychological perspectives on cultures, but of the potential of adapting and applying psychotherapeutic techniques to enhancing cultural harmony—indeed, of using such adapted techniques to healing cultures traumatized by their histories and weighed painfully down by the collective self-interpretations erected upon those histories.

That later step is a step I call upon readers to take, the step embodied in the term 'existential multiculturalism.' For multiculturalism is not a somehow extra human condition, an abstract social phenomenon. It is our day-to-day reality, our milieu, our environment, our collective destiny, our living experience.

This extra dimension, this spiritual dimension, in no way invalidates the life of the mind or the scientific process; it completes it. What I call Cultural Intelligence is a necessary and inevitable extension of both cultural competence and existential multiculturalism. It is a way of being and thinking. It is an extension that is often already unconsciously present in those who practice cultural competence. I argue that seeking and practicing its conscious presence is the missing element needed for cultural competence to flourish to its complete fulfillment.

In the encounter between a person of one culture and another, there are many uncertain moments—moments of fear, curiosity, pleasure, suspicion, wonder, hope. Moments of rejection and conflict, and moments of harmonious alignment. Moments that can devolve into hatred—or ascend to love.

Cultural intelligence is the moment of that ascent, that leap, the moment when our cultural competence reaches its fulfillment and goes beyond itself to thoughtfully embrace rather than thoughtlessly repulse such otherness; to dance, wordlessly, rather than exploit selfishly as we remain in our corners 'throwing sticks and stones.' It is an encounter not of mere tolerance but of richness and joy—a unity of intellect and spirit— the silence encounter between self and other that is overflowing with being. It is a doorway open to us all. What I call cultural intelligence points to that door.

References

References

Aigner, P. (2014). Ethnic diversity management in theory and practice. Journal of Diversity Management, 9(2), 111. doi:10.19030/jdm.v9i2.8976 Aleksandrov, D. S., Bowen, A. R., & Colker, J. (2016). Parent training and cultural considerations. Journal of Individual Psychology, 72(2), 77-89. doi:10.1353/jip.2016.0007

Alexander, J. C. (2013). Struggling over the mode of incorporation: Backlash against multiculturalism in Europe. Ethnic and Racial Studies, 36(4), 531-556. doi:1 0.1080/01419870.2012.752515

Althusser, L., Étienne Balibar, & Brewster, B. (1997). Reading Capital. Verso.

Ambroise, L., Pantin-Sohier, G., Valette-Florence, P., & Pierre, A. N. (2014). From endorsement to celebrity co-branding: Personality transfer. Journal of Brand Management, 21(4), 273-285. doi:10.1057/bm.2014.7

Antze, P. (2012). New departures in Anthropology: Psychotherapy as culture. Cambridge University Press.

Appe, S., Rubaii, N., & Stamp, K. (2016). International service learning in public and nonprofit management education. Journal of Nonprofit Education and Leadership, 6(1), 3-24. doi:10.18666/JNEL-2016-V6-I1-7200

Amoah, James. (2019). Devil In The Chain. Pascal Editions. https://www.amazon.com//dp/0989085546

Amoah, James. (2021). Chaotic Butterfly. Pascal Editions. https://www.amazon.com//dp/0989085546

Arnautovic, J. (2015). Serbian musical festivals in the 2000s as sites of intercultural dialogues. New Sound: International Journal of Music, 45(1), 224-227. Retrieved from   http://academicguides.waldenu.edu/library/ EBSCO

Asraf, R. M., & Brewer, J. K. (2004). Conducting tests of hypotheses: The need for an adequate sample size. Australian Educational Researcher, 31(1), 79-94. doi:10.1007/BF03216806

Atwater, M. M., Butler, M. B., Freeman, T. B., Carlton, P., & Eileen, R. (2013). An examination of Black science teacher educators' experiences with multicultural education, equity, and social justice. Journal of Science Teacher Education, 24(8), 1273-1313. doi:10.1007/s10972-013-9358-8

Awad, G. (2014). Motivation, persistence, and cross-cultural awareness: A study of college students learning foreign languages. Academy of Educational

Leadership Journal, 18(4), 97-116. Retrieved from http://academicguides.waldenu.edu/library/EBSCO

Badcock, C. R. (1992). Essential Freud (2nd ed.). Blackwell.

Bangwayo-Skeete, P. F., & Zikhali, P. (2013). Explaining self-declared social tolerance for human diversity in Latin America and the Caribbean. Forum for Social Economics, 42(2-3), 181-206. doi:10.1080/07360932.2012.714713

Banks, J. A., & McGee-Banks, C. A. (2010). Multicultural education: Issues and perspectives (7th Ed.). Hoboken, NJ: John Wiley & Sons, Inc.

Baudrillard, J. (1995). The Gulf War Did Not Take Place (P. Patton, Trans.). Indiana University Press.

Bell, P. (2010). Confronting Theory: The psychology of cultural studies. Intellect.

Benedict, R. (2019). Patterns Of Culture. Routledge.

Benahnia, A. (2015). Enriching educational policy makers & educator's intercultural competence via global conferences: An example of a SOE Global Conference in India. Economic and Social Development: Book of Proceedings, 2-9. Retrieved from http://academicguides.waldenu.edu/library/EBSCO

Bennett, M. J., & Bennett, M. J. (1993). Intercultural sensitivity. Principles of training and development. Portland, OR: Portland State University.

Besnoy, K. D., Maddin, E., Steele, E., & Eisenhardt, S. (2015). The friendship journey: Developing global understanding in the middle grades. Journal of Catholic Education, 18(2), 44-73. doi:10.15365/joce.1802042015

Bidee, J., Vantilborgh, T., Pepermans, R., Huybrechts, G., Willems, J., Jegers, M., & Hofmans, J. (2013). Autonomous motivation stimulates volunteers' work effort: A self-determination theory approach to volunteerism. Voluntas, 24(1), 32-47. doi:10.1007/s11266-012-9269-x

Bjork, Daniel W. (2013). B. F. Skinner: A Life. ISBN 9781557984166.

Bloch, Ernst(1989). The Utopian function of art and literature: Selected essays (J. Zipes & F. Mecklenburg, Trans.). MIT Press.

Bloch, Ernst (1995). The Principle of Hope. (Studies in Contemporary German Social Thought) (Volume 1). Neville Plaice (Translator), Stephen Plaice (Translator), Paul Knight (Translator). The MIT Press; Reprint edition.

Bloch, Ernst (1995). The Principle of Hope. (Studies in Contemporary German Social Thought) (Volume 2). Neville Plaice (Translator), Stephen Plaice (Translator).

The MIT Press; Reprint edition.

Bloch, Ernst (1995). The Principle of Hope. (Studies in Contemporary German Social Thought) (Volume 3). Neville Plaice (Translator), Stephen Plaice (Translator), Paul Knight (Translator). The MIT Press; Reprint edition.

Bloch, Ernst (2000). The Spirit of Utopia. Anthony A. Nassar (Translator). Meridian Press.

Blomberg, G., Sherin, M. G., Renkl, A., Glogger, I., & Seidel, T. (2014). Understanding video as a tool for teacher education: Investigating instructional strategies to promote reflection. Instructional Science, 42(3), 443-463. doi:10.1007/s11251-013-9281-6

Bloomquist, C. (2015). Reflecting on reflection as a critical component in service learning. Journal of Education for Library and Information Science, 56(2), 169- 172. doi:10.12783/issn.2328-2967/56/2/1

Boldyrev, I. A. (2015). Ernst Bloch and his contemporaries: Locating Utopian messianism. Bloomsbury Academic.

Bolman, L. G., & Deal, T. E. (2013). Reframing organizations: Artistry, choice, & leadership (5th Ed.). San Francisco, CA: Jossey-Bass.

Bringselius, L. (2014). Employee objections to organizational change: A framework for addressing management responses. Organizational Development Journal, 32(1), 41-54. Retrieved from http://academicguides.waldenu.edu/library/EBSCO

Brisebois, K. A., & Gonzalez-Prendes, A. (2014). My journey toward anti-oppressive work in child welfare. Reflections: Narratives of Professional Helping, 20(2), 26- 31. Retrieved from http://academicguides.waldenu.edu/library/SocINDEX

Bruno, D. M., Imperato, P. S., & Szarek, M. (2014). The correlation between global health experiences in low-income countries on choice of primary care residencies for graduates of an urban US Medical School. Journal of Urban Health, 91(2), 394-402. doi:10.1007/s11524-013-9829-4

Burnham, C. (2018). Does the internet have an unconscious? : Slavoj Žižek and digital culture: Slavoj zizek and digital culture. Bloomsbury Academic

Burhansstipanov, L., Krebs, L. U., Harjo, L., Watanabe-Galloway, S., & Pingatore, N. (2014). Providing community education: Lessons learned from native patient investigators. Journal of Cancer Education, 29(3), 596-606. doi:10.1007/s13187-014-0690-2

Butler-Barnes, S. T., Chavous, T. M., Hurd, N., & Varner, F. (2013). African American adolescents' academic persistence: A strengths-based approach. Journal of Youth and Adolescence, 42(9), 1443-1458. doi:10.1007/

s10964-013-9962-0

Buyse, A. (2014). Dangerous expressions: The ECHR, violence and free speech. The International and Comparative Law Quarterly, 63(2), 491-503. doi:10.1017/S0020589314000104

Cadeddu, F. (2015). A call to action: John Courtney Murray, S. J., and the renewal of American democracy. The Catholic Historical Review, 101(3), 530-553. doi:10.1353/cat.2015.0114

Cambridge, J. (2012). Internationalizing teacher education in the United States. The International Schools Journal, 32(1), 82-85. Retrieved from http://academicguides.waldenu.edu/library/GoogleScholar

Canning, J., & Found, P.A. (2015). The effects of resistance in organizational change programmes: A study of a lean transformation. International Journal of Quality and Service Sciences, 7(2/3), 274-295. doi:10.1108/IJQSS-02-2015-0018

Cannon, A. M. (2012). Virtually audible in diaspora: The transnational negotiation of Vietnamese traditional music. Journal of Vietnamese Studies, 7(3), 122-156. doi:10.1525/vs.2012.7.3.122

Carano, K. (2013). An autoethnography: Constructing (& interpreting) cross-cultural awareness through the mind of a Peace Corps volunteer. The Qualitative Report,

18(18), 1-15. Retrieved from http://www.nova.edu/ssss/ QR/QR18/carano35.pdf

Carrara , Kester. (2018). Radical Behaviorism and Cultural Analysis. Publisher: Springer. ISBN: 9783319743004, 3319743007, eText ISBN: 9783319743011, 3319743015

Casey, J. E. (2014). A personal journey of volunteerism. Canadian Psychology, 55(1), 34-37. doi:10.1037/a00355562

Castleberry, A. (2014). NVIVO 10 [software program]. American Journal of Pharmaceutical Education, 78(1), 1-2. doi:10.5688/ajpe78125

Charles, L., Maltby, H., Abrams, S., Shea, J., Brand, G., & Nicol, P. (2014). Expanding worldview: Australian nursing students' experience of cultural immersion in India. Contemporary Nurse: A Journal for the Australian Nursing Profession, 48(1), 67-75. doi:10.1080/10376178.2 014.11081928

Chiner, E., Cardona-Molto, M. C., & Puerta, J. M. G. (2015). Teachers' beliefs about diversity: An analysis from a personal and professional perspective. Journal of New Approaches in Educational Research, 4(1), 18-24A. doi:10.7821/naer.2015.1.113

Chrobot-Mason, D. & Leslie, J. B. (2012). The role of multicultural competence and emotional intelligence in managing diversity. Psychologist-Manager Journal,

15(4), 219-236. doi:10.1080/10887156.2012.730442

Clark, P., & Zygmunt, E. (2014). A close encounter with personal bias: Pedagogical implications for teacher education. The Journal of Negro Education, 83(2), 147-161. doi:10.7709/jnegroeducation.83.2.0147

Colvin, C., Volet, S., & Fozdar, F. (2014). Local university students and intercultural interactions: Conceptualizing culture, seeing diversity and experiencing interactions. Higher Education Research & Development, 33(3), 440-455. doi:10.1080/07294360.2013.841642

Constantin, E. C., Cohen-Vida, M., & Popescu, A. V. (2015). Developing cultural awareness. Procedia Social and Behavioral Sciences, 191, 696-699. doi:10.1016/j.sbspro.2015.04.228

Constantin, E. C. (2012). Gaining the young generation's attention. Procedia Social and Behavioral Sciences, 46, 4130-4135. doi:10.1016/j.sbspro.2012.06.212

Chu, M. (2014). Preparing tomorrow's Early Childhood educators: Observe and reflect about culturally responsive teachers. YC Young Children, 69(2), 82-87. Retrieved from http://academicguides.waldenu.edu/library/GoogleScholar

Creswell, J. W. (2013). Qualitative inquiry & research design: Choosing among five approaches (3rd Ed.). Thousand Oaks, CA: Sage Publications, Inc.

Cui, Q. (2013). Global-mindedness and intercultural competence: A quantitative study of pre-service teachers (Doctoral dissertation). Available from ProQuest Dissertations and Theses database. (UMI No. 358995).

Dahlman, H. (2013). The journey toward cross-cultural competence is never-ending. Momentum, 44(3), 27-29. Retrieved from http://academicguides.waldenu.edu/library/EBSCO

Darling-Hammond, L. (1996). Securing the right to learn: Policy and practice for powerful teaching and learning. Educational Researcher, 35(7), 13-24. doi:10.3102/0013189X035007013

Das Neves, J. C., & Mele, D. (2013). Managing ethically cultural diversity: Learning from Thomas Aquinas. Journal of Business Ethics, 116, 769-780. doi:10.1007/s10551-013-1820-1

Dawidziuk, M., Boboryko-Hocazade, J., & Mazur, B. (2012). The intercultural competencies of the managers and organization in the global world. Managerial Challenges of the Contemporary Society, 3, 117-120. Retrieved from http://academicguides.waldenu.edu/library/EBSCO

DeCesare, J. A. (2014). The mass market and consumer tools. Library Technology Reports, 50(2), 33-39. Retrieved from http://academicguides.waldenu.edu/library/EBSCO

Deleuze, Gilles & Boundas, C. V. (1993). The Deleuze reader. Columbia University Press.

Deleuze, Gilles & Hand, S. (2016). Foucault. University Of Minnesota Press.

Delphin-Rittmon, M. E., Andres-Hyman, R., Flanagan, E. H., & Davidson, L. (2013). Seven essential strategies for promoting and sustaining systemic cultural competence. Psychiatric Quarterly, 84, 53-64. doi:10.1007/s11126-012-9226-2

Denson, N., & Bowman, N. (2013). University diversity and preparation for a global society: The role of diversity in shaping intergroup attitudes and civic outcomes. Studies in Higher Education, 38(4), 555-570. doi:10.1080/03075079.2011.584971

DeProw, S. L. (2014). Effects of multicultural group projects on domestic students' intercultural competence (Doctoral dissertation). Available from ProQuest Dissertations and Theses database. (UMI No. 362855).

Devereux, P. (2008). International volunteering for development and sustainability: Outdated paternalism or a radical response to globalization. Development in Practice, 18(3), 357-370. doi:10.1080/09614520802030409

Donovan, D. M., Thomas, L. R., Sigo, R. L., Price, L. A., & Lonczak, H. (2015). Healing of the canoe: Preliminary results of a culturally grounded intervention to prevent substance abuse and promote tribal identity for native youth in two Pacific Northwest tribes. American Indian and Alaska Native Mental Health Research (Online), 22(1), 42-76. Retrieved from http://academicguides. waldenu.edu/library/EBSCO

Drassinower, A. (2003). Freud's theory of culture: Eros, loss, and politics. Rowman & Littlefield.

Dumitrescu, C. I., Lie, I. R., & Dobrescu, R. M. (2014). Leading multiculturalism teams. FAIMA Business & Management Journal, 2(4), 43-54. Retrieved from http:// academicguides.waldenu.edu/library/EBSCO

Dunagan, P. B., Kimble, L. P., Gunby, S. S., & Andrews, M. M. (2014). Attitudes of prejudice as a predictor of cultural competence among baccalaureate nursing students. Journal of Nursing Education, 53(6), 320-328. doi:10.3928/01484834-20140521-13

Dutt, S., & Kumari, P. (2015). Relationship between socio-economic status and academic achievement towards environmental consciousness. Indian Journal of Positive Psychology, 6(4), 426-428. Retrieved from http:// academicguides.waldenu.edu/library/EBSCO

Edwards, O. A. (2014). Cross-cultural factorial validity of the academic motivation scale. Cross-Cultural Management, 21(1), 104-125. doi:10.1108/CCM-11-2011-0100

Epstein, R. A. (2014). Public accommodations under the Civil Rights Act of 1964: Why freedom of association counts as a human right. Stanford Law Review, 66(6), 1241-1291. Retrieved from http://academicguides.waldenu.edu/library/ProQuest

Nye, Robert D. (1979). What Is B. F. Skinner Really Saying? Englewood Cliffs, NJ: Prentice-Hall.

Exton, M., & Enloe, W. (2014). Lessons from Hiroshima: Building cultures of peace in international education. The International Schools Journal, 32(1), 20-26. Retrieved from http://academicguides.waldenu.edu/library/EBSCO

Frankfort-Nachmias, C., & Nachmias, D. (2008). Research methods in the social sciences (7th Ed.). New York, NY: Worth Publishers.

Friedman, H., Glover, G., Sims, E., Culhane, E., & Guest, M. (2013). Cross-cultural competence: Performance-based assessment and training. Organization Development Journal, 31(2), 18-30. Retrieved from http://academicguides.waldenu.edu/library/EBSCO

Fuery, P., & Mansfield, N. (2000). Cultural studies and critical theory: Concepts and controversies (2nd ed.). OUP Australia.

Gackowski, T. (2014). What power resides in the mass

media? Typology of media's power – a proposal. Politicke Vedy, 4, 109-141. Retrieved from http://academicguides. waldenu.edu/library/GoogleScholar

Galante, A. (2014). Developing EAL learners' intercultural sensitivity through a digital literacy project. TESL Canada Journal, 32(1), 53-66. doi:10.18806/tesl. v32i1.1199

Gandhi, M. (2011). All men are brothers : life & thoughts of Mahatma Gandhi as told in his own words. Rajpal & Sons.

Gandolfi, F. (2012). A conceptual discussion of transformational leadership and intercultural competence. Revista de Management Comparat International, 13(4), 522-534. Retrieved from http:// academicguides.waldenu.edu/library/EBSCO

Garcia, H. A., & Ramirez, N. (2015). Why race and culture matters in schools: Closing the achievement gap in America's classrooms. The Journal of Negro Education, 84(1), 98-101. Retrieved from http://academicguides. waldenu.edu/library/EBSCO

Garrett-Rucks, P. (2013). A discussion-based online approach to fostering deep cultural inquiry in an introductory language course. Foreign Language Annals, 46(2), 191-212. doi:10.1111/flan.12026

Gerhauser, P. T. (2014). Framing Arab-Americans and

Muslims in US Media. Sociological Viewpoints, 30(1), 7. Retrieved from http://academicguides.waldenu.edu/ library/SocINDEX

Gibson, C., Hardy, J. H., & Buckley, M. R. (2014). Understanding the role of networking in organizations. Career Development International, 19(2), 146-161. doi:10.1108/CDI-09-2013-0111

Gill, N., Johnstone, P., & Williams, A. (2012). Towards a geography of tolerance: Post- politics and political forms of toleration. Political Geography, 8, 509-519. doi:10.1016/j.polgeo.2012.10.008

Giroux, H. A. (2005). Border crossings: Cultural workers and the politics of education (2nd Ed.). New York, NY: Routledge Publishing.

González-Rodríguez, M. R., Díaz-Fernández, M. C., Pawlak, M., & Simonetti, B. (2013). Perceptions of students' university of corporate social responsibility. Quality & Quantity, 47(4), 2361-2377. doi:10.1007/s11135-012-9781-5

Graham, S. (2014). Cultural exchange in a Black Atlantic Web: South African literature, Langston Hughes, and Negritude. Twentieth Century Literature, 60(4), 481-512, 555. Retrieved from http://academicguides.waldenu.edu/library/ProQuest

Gramsci, A. (1971). Selections from the prison

notebooks of Antonio Gramsci. International Publishers.

Grass, S. (2014). An evaluation of an international service experience and students' intercultural competence (Doctoral dissertation). Available from ProQuest Dissertations and Theses database. (UMI No. 3681724).

Gruenewald, D. A. (2003). The best of both worlds: A critical pedagogy of place. Educational Researcher, 32(4), 3-12. doi:10.3102/0013189X032004003

Guillen-Nieto, V., & Aleson-Carbonell, M. (2012). Serious games and learning effectiveness: The case of It's a Deal! Computer & Education, 58(1), 435-448. doi:10.1016/j.compedu.2011.07.015

Guo, M., & Sun, Y. (2013). Cross-cultural communication competence for Science and engineering college students: Survey & proposal. Theory and Practice in Language Studies, 3(7), 1136-1142. doi:10.4304/tpls.3.7.1136-1142

Gwyer, J., & Hack, L. (2014). In search of cultural competence. Journal of Physical Therapy Education, 28(1), 3. Retrieved from http://academicguides.waldenu.edu/library/SocINDEX

Haffar, W., & Crenshaw, S. (2012/2013). The faces of peace: NGOS, global education, and university curricula. Peace Research, 44/45(2/1), 193-209, 222-223. Retrieved from http://www.jstor.org/stable/24429465

Harris, P. C., Hines, E. M., Kelly, D. D., Williams, D. J., & Bagley, B. (2014). Promoting the academic engagement and success of black male student-athletes. The High School Journal, 97(3), 180-195. doi:10.1353/hsj.2014.0000

Harris, R. (2012). 'Purpose' as a way of helping White trainee: History teachers engage with diversity issues. Education Sciences, 2(4), 218-241. doi:10.3390/educsci2040218

Hart, P. (2012). The battle for the mind: War and peace in the era of mass communication. Journalism & Mass Communication Educator, 67(3), 302-304. doi:10.1177/1077695812450555

Hauk, E., & Immordino, G. (2014). Parents, television, and cultural change. Economic Journal, 124(159), 1040-1065. doi:10.1111/ecoj.12078

Harris, M. (2002). Cultural Materialism. The Struggle for a Science of Culture. Altamira Press.

Hayward, L. M., Venere, K., & Pallais, A. (2015). Enhancements to an international service-learning model: Integration of program alumni and global stakeholder feedback. Journal of Physical Therapy Education, 29(21), 43-53. Retrieved from http://academicguides.waldenu.edu/library/SocINDEX

Heidari, A., Ketabi, S., & Zonoobi, R. (2014). The role of culture through the eyes of different approaches to and methods of foreign language teaching. Journal of Intercultural Communication, 34. Retrieved from http://academicguides.waldenu.edu/library/SocINDEX

Hervik, P. (2012). Ending tolerance as a solution to incompatibility: The Danish "crisis of multiculturalism." European Journal of Cultural Studies, 15, 211-225. doi:10.1177/1367549411432024

Heselmeyer, R. J. (2014). First contact: Initial responses to cultural disequilibrium in a short term teaching exchange program (Doctoral dissertation). Available from ProQuest Dissertations and Theses database. (UMI No. 3637328).

Hester, R. J. (2012). The promise and paradox of cultural competence. HEC Forum, 24, 279–291. doi:10.1007/s10730-012-9200-2

Hill, I., & Saxton, S. (2014). The International Baccalaureate (IB) Programme: An international gateway to higher education and beyond. Higher Learning Research Communications, 4(3), 42-52. Retrieved from http://academicguides.waldenu.edu/library/SocINDEX

Horn, A. S., & Fry, G. W. (2013). Promoting global citizenship through study abroad: The influence of program destination, type, and duration on the propensity for development volunteerism. Voluntas,

24(4), 1159-1179. doi:10.1007/s11266-012-9304-y

Intolubbe-Chmil, L., Spreen, C. A., & Swap, R. J. (2013). Transformative learning: Participant perspectives on international experiential education. Journal of Research in International Education, 11(2), 65-180. doi:10/1177/1475240912448041

Janesick, V. J. (2011). Stretching exercises for qualitative researchers (3rd Ed.). Thousand Oaks: CA: Sage Publications.

Jansson, N. (2013). Organizational change as practice: A critical analysis. Journal of Organizational Change Management, 26(6), 1003-1019. doi:10.1108/JOCM-09-2012-0152

Jauhar, V., & Munjal, S. (2015). Fairs and festivals in India: The cultural and economic potential. Worldwide Hospitality and Tourism Themes, 74(4), 324-330. doi:10.1108/WHA TT-03-2015-0012

Jobe, K. (2012). Disaster relief in post-earthquake Haiti: Unintended consequences of humanitarian volunteerism. Travel Medicine and Infectious Disease, 9(1), 1-5. doi:10.1016/j.tmaid.2010.10.006

Kickett, M., Hoffman, J., & Flavell, H. (2014). A model for large-scale, interprofessional, compulsory cross-cultural education with an indigenous focus. Journal of Allied Health, 43(1), 38-44. Retrieved from http://

academicguides.waldenu.edu/library/SocINDEX

Killion, D. T. (2013). Why UNESCO is a critical tool for twenty-first century diplomacy. The Fletcher Forum of World Affairs, 37(2), 7-14. Retrieved from http://academicguides.waldenu.edu/library/EBSCO

King, M. L., & Clayborne, C. (1997). The papers of Martin Luther King, Jr. Vol. 3, Birth of a new age, December 1955-December 1956. University Of California Press.

Kirschenbaum, H. (1990). The Carl Rogers Reader. Little, Brown.

Koehn, P. H., & Rosenau, J. N. (2002). Transnational competence in an emergent epoch. International Studies Perspectives, 3(2), 105-127. doi:10.1111/1528-3577.00084

Korsmo, J., & Barrett, W., Friesen, S., & Finnley, L. (2012). Mission possible: The efforts of the International Baccalaureate to align mission and vision with daily practice. The International School Journal, 32(1), 29-39. Retrieved from http://academicguides.waldenu.edu/library/ProQuest

Korstvedt, B. M. (2010). Listening for utopia in Ernst bloch's musical philosophy. Cambridge University Press.

Koskinen, L., Taylor-Kelly, H., Bergknut, E., Lundberg, P., Muir, N., Olt, H., Richardson, E., Sairanen,

R., & Vlieger, L. D. (2012). European higher health care education curriculum development of a cultural framework. Journal of Transcultural Nursing, 23(3), 313-319. doi:10.1177/1043659612441020

Lacy, S., Wildman, S. S. Fico, F., Bergan, D., & Baldwin, T. (2013). How radio news uses sources to cover local government news and factors affecting source use. Journalism and Mass Communication Quarterly, 90(3), 457-477. doi:10.1177/1077699013493790

Lakshman, C. (2013). Biculturalism and attributional complexity: Cross-cultural leadership effectiveness. Journal of International Business Studies, 44(9), 922- 940. doi:10.1057/jibs.2013.36

Lash, M., & Ratcliffe, M. (2014). The journey of an African American teacher before and after Brown v. Board of Education. The Journal of Negro Education, 83(3), 327- 337, 426. doi:10.7709/jnegroeducation.83.3.0327

Lauring, J., & Selmer, J. (2012). Openness to diversity, trust and conflict in multicultural organizations. Journal of Management and Organization, 18(6), 795-806. doi:10.1017/S1833367200000444

Laws, T., & Chilton, J. A. (2013). Ethics, cultural competence, and the changing face of America. Pastoral Psychology, 62, 175–188. doi:10.1007/s11089-012-0428-1

Lebedeva, N. M., & Galyapina, V. N. (2016). Is

multiculturalism in Russia possible? Intercultural relations in North Ossetia-Alania. Psychology in Russia, 9(1), 24-40. doi:10.11621/pir.2016.0102

Lee, S. (2012). Knowing myself to know others: Preparing preservice teachers for diversity through multicultural autobiography. Multicultural Education, 20(1), 38- 41. Retrieved from http://academicguides.waldenu.edu/library/ProQuest

Liu, L. B., & Milman, N. B. (2014). Developing glocally informed diversity and equity discourses: Examining inequity via autobiographical reflection. Teacher Development, 18(4), 546-561. doi:10.1080/13664 530.2014.946151

Lobb, P. M. (2012). Making multicultural education personal. Multicultural Perspectives,

14(4), 229-233. doi:10.1080/15210960.2012.725336

Lott, J. L, 11. (2013). Predictors of civic values: Understanding student-level and institutional-level effects. Journal of College Student Development, 54(1), 1-16. doi:10.1353/csd.2013.0002

Macnamara, J. (2014). Organisational listening: A vital missing element in public communication and the public sphere. Asia Pacific Public Relations Journal, 15(1), 89-108. Retrieved from http://www.pria.com.au/journal

Madyun, N., Williams, S. M., McGee, E. O., & Milner, H. R, IV. (2013). On the importance of African-American faculty in higher education: Implications and recommendations. Journal of Educational Foundations, 27(3/4), 65-84. Retrieved from http://academicguides. waldenu.edu/library/ProQuest

Maher, Z., Khorasgani, A. R., & Hashemianfar, S. A. (2015). Investigating citizens' experience of Public Communication of Science (PCS) and the role of media in contributing to this experience (A case study on Isfahan citizens). Global Media Journal, 13(24), 1-30. Retrieved from http://academicguides.waldenu.edu/ library/GoogleScholar

Marcuse, H. (2008). One-dimensional man : studies in the ideology of advanced industrial society. Routledge. (Original work published 1964)

Marx, E. (1999). Breaking through culture shock: What you need to succeed in international business. Nicholas Brealey Publishing.

Marx, Karl. (2018). Capital Vol. 1, 2, & 3: Complete and Unabridged Edition in One Volume. Jake E. Stief (Editor), Ernest Unterman (Translator), Samuel Moor (Translator), Edward Aveling (Translator). Independently published: https://www.amazon.com//dp/1791968465.

Matteliano, M. A., & Stone, J. H. (2014). Cultural competence education in university rehabilitation programs. Journal of Cultural Diversity, 21(3), 112-118. Retrieved from http://academicguides.waldenu.edu/library/ProQuest

Mbemba, A. (2014). Challenges of teaching economics in international exchange programs. International Journal of Economics and Finance, 6(8), 68-77. doi:10.5539/ijef.v6n8p68

McLeod-Harrison, M. S. (2005). Repairing Eden: Humility, mysticism, and the existential problem of religious diversity. McGill-Queens University Press.

McLuhan, M., Fiore, Q., & Agel, J. (2001). The medium is the massage. Gingko Press.

McLuhan, Marshall. (1964). Understanding Media: The Extensions of Man. New York: McGraw-Hill.

McLuhan, M. (2015). Culture Is Our Business. Wipf & Stock.

McLuhan, M., & Fiore, Q. (1997). War and Peace in the Global Village. Wired Books.

McLuhan, M., Fiore, Q., & Agel, J. (2001). The medium is the massage. Gingko Press.

McLuhan, M., & McLuhan, C. (2011). The Gutenberg Galaxy. University of Toronto Press.

McLuhan, M., & McLuhan, E. (1992). Laws of media: The new science. University of Toronto Press.

Mendy, J. (2012). Employees' witnessed presence in changing organizations. AI & Society, 27(1), 149-156. doi:10.1007/s00146-011-0324-8

Merriam, S. B. (2009). Qualitative research: A guide to design and implementation. San Francisco: Jossey-Bass.

Meskell, L. (2013). UNESCO and the fate of World Heritage Indigenous Peoples Council of Experts (WHIPCOE). International Journal of Cultural Property, 20(2), 155- 174. doi:10.1017/S0940739113000039

Miles, M. B., Huberman, A. M., & Saldana, J. (2014). Qualitative data analysis: Amethods sourcebook (3rd Ed.). Thousand Oaks, CA: SAGE Publications.

Miller, V. (2020). Understanding digital culture. Sage.

Mills, C. (2013). Developing pedagogies in pre-service teachers to cater for diversity: Challenges and ways forward in initial teacher education. International Journal of Pedagogies & Learning, 8(3), 219-228. doi:10.5172/ijpl.2013.8.3.219

Mills, C. Wrigh t& Irving Louis Horowitz. (1971). The new sociology : essays in social science and social theory in honor of C. Wright Mills. Oxford University Press.

Miche, Particia M. (2002). After 9/11--Paths To Peace. Kosmos Journal: Spring/Summer 2002. https://www. kosmosjournal.org/article/after-911-paths-to-peace/

Morris, S., Wilmot, A., Hill, M., Ockenden, N., Payne, S. (2013). A narrative literature review of the contribution of volunteerism in end-of-life care services. Palliative Medicine, 27(5), 429-436. doi:10.1177/0269216312453608

Motlagh, N. E., Hassan, S. B., Bolong, J. B., & Osman, M. N. (2013). Role of journalists' gender, work experience, and education in ethical decision making. Asian Social Science, 9(9), 1-10. Retrieved from http:// academicguides.waldenu.edu/library/ProQuest

Mouffe, C. (2020). Return Of The Political. Verso Books.

Camila Muchon de Melo & Júlio C. de Rose. (2013). The Concept of Culture in Skinnerian Radical Behaviorism: Debates and Controversies. European Journal of Behavior Analysis, 14:2, 321-328, doi:10.1080/15021149.2013.11434464

Mujtaba, B. G. (2013). Ethnic diversity, distrust and corruption in Afghanistan. Equality, Diversity and Inclusion: An International Journal, 32(3), 245-261. doi:10.1108/EDI-12-2012-0113

Murmu, N. (2014). Cultural diversity in global workforce: Issues and challenges. Review of HRM, 3, 67-72. Retrieved from http://academicguides.waldenu.edu/library/ProQuest

Nagy, E. (2014). Sound and image-communication by text in audio-visual mass-media of Romania. International Journal of Communication Research, 4(2), 25-29. Retrieved from http://academicguides.waldenu.edu/library/ProQuest

NAME. (2015). About NAME. Retrieved from http://www.name.org

Nassar-McMillan, S. C. (2014). A framework for cultural competence, advocacy, and social justice: Applications for global multiculturalism and diversity. International Journal for Educational and Vocational Guidance, 14(1), 103-118. doi:10.1007/s10775-014-9265-3

Nasir, N., & Ahmad, J. H. (2013). Effective environmental communication: A case study of environmental Non-Government Organization (ENGO) in Malaysia. Journal of Social and Development Sciences, 4(6), 242-248. Retrieved from http://academicguides.waldenu.edu/library/ProQuest

Naour, Paul. (2009.) E.O. Wilson and B. F. Skinner: A Dialogue Between Sociobiology and Radical Behaviorism. Developments in primatology: Progress and prospects. Publisher: Springer-Verlag.

Neal, Z. P., & Neal, J. W. (2014). The (in) compatibility of diversity and sense of community. American Journal of Community Psychology, 53(1-2), 1-12. doi:10.1007/s10464-013-9608-0

Nelson, C., & Grossberg, L. (1988). Marxism and the interpretation of culture (C. Nelson & L. Grossberg, Eds.). Palgrave Macmillan.

Neville, & Horowitz, M. (2021). The Power of Awareness. G&D Media.

Nhất Hạnh, Thích, & Ellsberg, R. (2008). The Essential Thich Nhat Hanh : Thich Nhat Hanh. Darton Longman & Todd.

Nilay, S. (2014). Navigating the international academic job market. PS, Political Science & Politics, 47(4), 845-848. doi:10.1017/S1049096514001152

Norton, D., & Marks-Maran, D. (2014). Developing cultural sensitivity and awareness in nursing overseas. Nursing Standard, 28(44), 39-43. doi:10.7748/ns.28.44.39.e8417

Norviliene, A. (2012). Self-development of intercultural competence in academic exchange programmers: Students' attitude. Social Sciences, 75(1), 58-65. doi:10.5755/j01.ss.75.1.1592

Oginde, David A. (2013). Effects of ethnicity and

intercultural competence on follower trust, leader-member exchange, and perceptions of organizational justice (Doctoral Dissertation). Available from ProQuest Dissertations and Theses database. (UMI No. 3570904).

O'Hara, B. J., & Bauman, A. E., Phongsavan, P. (2012). Using mass-media communications to increase population usage of Australia's get healthy information and coaching service? BMC Public Health, 12, 762. Retrieved from http://academicguides.waldenu.edu/library/GoogleScholar

O'Reilly, F. L., Matt, J. L., McCaw, W. P., Kero, P., & Stewart, C. (2014). International study tour groups. Journal of Education and Learning, 3(1), 52-59. Retrieved from http://academicguides.waldenu.edu/library/ProQuest

Pajtinka, E. (2014). Cultural diplomacy in theory and practice of contemporary international relations. Politicke Vedy, 4, 95-108. Retrieved from http://academicguides.waldenu.edu/library/EBSCO

Palmer, S., & Moodley, R. (Eds.). (2006). Race, culture and psychotherapy: Critical perspectives in multicultural practice. Brunner-Routledge.

Palmieri, D. (2012). An institution standing the test of time? A review of 150 years of the history of the International Committee of the Red Cross. International Review of the Red Cross, Suppl. ICRC: 150 Years of

Humanitarian Action, 94(888), 1273-1298. doi:10.1017/S1816283113000039

Paris, D. (2012). Culturally sustaining pedagogy: A needed change in stance, terminology, and practice. Educational Researcher, 41(3), 93-97. doi:10.3102/0013189X12441244

Park, K., Caine, V., & Wimmer, R. (2014). The experiences of advanced placement and international baccalaureate diploma program participants: A systematic review of qualitative research. Journal of Advanced Academics, 25(2), 129-153. doi:10.1177/1932202X14532258

Patton, M. Q. (2002). Qualitative research & evaluation methods (3rd Ed.). Thousand Oaks, CA: Sage Publications, Inc.

Peckenpaugh, K. (2013). Becoming transcultural: Maximizing study abroad (Doctoral dissertation). Available from ProQuest Dissertations and Theses database. (UMI No.3587286).

Petrus, R., & Bocos, M. (2012). Teaching English through cultural lenses: A perspective on initial teacher training programs. The Journal of Linguistic and Intercultural Education, 5, 95-107, 215-218. Retrieved from http://academicguides.waldenu.edu/library/ProQuest

Pettigrew, T. (1991). Normative theory in intergroup

relations: Explaining both harmony and conflict. Psychology and Developing Societies, 3, 3-16. doi:10.1177/097133369100300102

Pitsakis, K., Biniari, M. G., & Kuin, T. (2012). Resisting change: Organizational decoupling through identity construction perspective. Journal of Organizational Change Management, 25(6), 835-852. doi:10.1108/09534811211280591

Potgieter, F. J., Van der Walt, J. L., & Wolhuter, C. C. (2014). Towards understanding (religious) (in) tolerance in education. Hervormde Teologiese Studies, 70(3), 1-8. Retrieved from http://academicguides.waldenu.edu/library/EBSCO

Qin, Y. (2012). Cross-cultural competence and its development. Theory and Practice in Language Studies, 2(1), 92-96. doi:10.4304/tpls.2.1.92-96

Quappe, S., & Cantatore, G. (2011). What is cultural awareness, anyway? How do I build it? Retrieved from http://academicguides.waldenu.edu/library/ProQuest

Radhakrishna, R. (2012). Macro and micro level challenges to program evaluation and accountability. Retrieved from http://www.jsaer.org/pdf/Vol50/50-00-091.pdf

Raghupathi, V. (2016). Changes in virtual team collaboration with modern collaboration tools.

Manager's Journal on Information Technology, 5(2), 5-13. Retrieved from http://academicguides.waldenu. edu/library/ProQuest

Raina, R., Roebuck, D. B., & Lee, C. E. (2014). An exploratory study of listening skills of professionals across different cultures. Digital Commons @ Kennesaw University. Retrieved from http://academicguides. waldenu.edu/library/GoogleScholar

Ralston, D. A., Egri, C. P., Furrer, O., Kuo, M., & Li, Y. (2014). Societal-level versus individual-level predictions of ethical behavior: A 48-society study of collectivism and individualism. Journal of Business Ethics, 122(2), 283-306. doi:10.1007/s10551-013-1744-9

Rattanamethawong, V., Sinthupinyo, S., & Chandrachai, A. (2014). An innovation system that can quickly respond to the needs of students and alumni. Procedia Social and Behavioral Sciences, 182, 645-652. doi:10.1016/j.sbspro.2015.04.801

Rearden, A. K. (2012). Recruitment and retention of Alaska natives into nursing: Elements enabling educational success. Journal of Cultural Diversity, 19(3), 72-8. Retrieved from http://academicguides.waldenu. edu/library/ProQuest

Reed, K., Goolsby, J. R., & Johnston, M. K. (2016). Extracting meaning and relevance from work: The potential connection between the listening environment and employee's organizational identification and commitment. Internal Journal of Business Communication, 53(3), 326-342. doi:10.1177/2329488414525465

Riviere, A. (2013). Challenging students on global issues, an interdisciplinary approach: Part 1. The International Schools Journal, 32(2), 16-25. Retrieved from http://academicguides.waldenu.edu/library/ProQuest

Roy, L. R. (2015). Salsa, soul, and spirit: Leadership for a multicultural age. Educational Studies, 51(4), 343-346. doi:10.1080/00131946.2015.1052441

Ruecker, T. (2013). The twenty-first century student. Academe, 99(3), 52-54. Retrieved from http://academicguides.waldenu.edu/library/EBSCO

Sanchez, P. (2014). Dignifying every day: Policies and practices that impact immigrant students. Language Arts, 91(5), 363-371. Retrieved from http://academicguides.waldenu.edu/library/ProQuest

Schoorman, D. (2014). How should researchers act in the context of social injustice? Reflections on the role of the researcher as a social justice leader. In International Handbook of Educational Leadership and Social (In) Justice, 217-232. Springer Netherlands. doi:10.1007/978-94-007-6555-9_13

Schultz, W. R. (2018). Genetic codes of culture?: The deconstruction of tradition by Kuhn, bloom, and Derrida. Routledge.

Seidman, I. (2013). Interviewing as qualitative research: A guide for researchers in education and social sciences (4th Ed.). New York, NY: Teachers College Press. Shaklee, B., & Merz, S. (2012). International communication competency for international educators. The International Schools Journal, 32(1), 13-20. Retrieved from http://academicguides.waldenu.edu/library/ EBSCO

Shelton, T. M. (2013). My crucible: The intercultural performance (Doctoral dissertation). Available from ProQuest Dissertations and Theses database. (UMI No. 3555196).

Shen, Z. (2015). Cultural competence models and cultural competence assessment instruments in nursing: A literature review. Journal of Transcultural Nursing, 26(3), 308-321. doi:10.1177/1043659614524790

Singh, N. K. (2012). Eastern and cross cultural management. Chicago, IL: Springer Science & Business Media

Skinner, B. F. The control of human behavior. (1955). Transactions of the New York Academy of Sciences. 17: 547-51. doi: 10.1111/J.2164-0947.1955.Tb02820.X

Skinner, B. F. Behaviorism at fifty. (1963). Science (New York, N.Y.). 140: 951-8. doi: 10.1097/00006199-196401310-00082

Skinner, B. F. The technology of teaching. (1963). Proceedings of the Royal Society of London. Series B, Biological Sciences. 162: 427-43. doi: 10.2307/1420451

Skinner, B. F. The phylogeny and ontogeny of behavior. Contingencies of reinforcement throw light on contingencies of survival in the evolution of behavior. (1966). Science (New York, N.Y.). 153: 1205-13. doi: 10.1126/science.153.3741.1205

Skinner, B. F. Contingencies of reinforcement in the design of a culture. (1966). Behavioral Science. 11: 159-66. doi: 10.1002/Bs.3830110302

Skinner, B. F. Letters. (1968). Science (New York, N.Y.). 160: 718. doi: 10.1126/science.160.3829.718-a

Skinner, B. F. (1971). Beyond Freedom and Dignity. New York: Knopf.

Skinner, B. F. (1981). Selection by consequences. Science (New York, N.Y.). 213: 501-4. PMID 7244649 doi: 10.1017/S0140525X0002673X

Skinner, B. F. (1981). How to discover what you have to say-a talk to students. The Behavior Analyst / Maba. 4: 1-7. Doi: 10.1007/Bf03391847

Skinner, B. F. (1986). What is wrong with daily life in the western world? American Psychologist, 1986, 41, 568-74.

Skinner, B. F. (1987). Upon Further Reflection. Englewood Cliffs, NJ: Prentice-Hall, 1987.

Skowronski, D. P., Othman, A. B., Siang, D. T., Han, G. L., & Yang, J. W. (2014). The outline of selected marital satisfaction factors in the intercultural couples based on the westerner and non-westerner relationships. Polish Psychological Bulletin, 45(3), 346-356. doi:10.2478/ppb-2014-0042

Small, M. W. (2014). Culture, values and integrity in contemporary society. Journal of Business Systems, Governance & Ethics, 9(2), 66-71. Retrieved from http://academicguides.waldenu.edu/library/EBSCO

Smadja, E. (2019). Freud and Culture. Routledge.

Souto-Manning, M. (2013). Teaching young children from immigrant and diverse families. YC Young Children, 68(4), 72-76, 78-80. Retrieved from http://academicguides.waldenu.edu/library/EBSCO

Spengler, Oswald & Anaconda Verlag Gmbh. (2017). Der Untergang des Abendlandes Umrisse einer Morphologie der Weltgeschichte. Köln Anaconda.

Stennis, K. B., Purnell, K., Perkins, E., & Fischle,

H. (2015). Lessons learned: Conducting culturally competent research and providing interventions with Black churches. Social Work & Christianity, 25(3), 332-349. Retrieved from http://academicguides.waldenu.edu/library/ProQuest

Stevens, S., & Miretzky, D. (2014). The foundations of teaching for diversity: What teachers tell us about transferable skills. Multicultural Education, 22(1), 30-40. Retrieved from http://academicguides.waldenu.edu/library/ProQuest

Stewart, A. C., Wilson, C. E., & Miles, A. K. (2014). Developing ethically & culturally- intelligent leaders through international service experiences. Journal of Leadership, Accountability and Ethics, 11(2), 115-127. Retrieved from http://academicguides.waldenu.edu/library/ProQuest

Subrick, J. R. (2015). Religion and the social order: Lessons from Smith, Hayek, and Smith. Journal of Markets and Morality, 18(2), 310-329. Retrieved from http://academicguides.waldenu.edu/library/ProQuest

Swirski, Peter. (2011). "How I Stopped Worrying and Loved Behavioural Engineering or Communal Life, Adaptations, and B.F. Skinner's Walden Two". American Utopia and Social Engineering in Literature, Social Thought, and Political History. New York, Routledge.

Tarc, P., & Beatty, L. (2012). The emergence of

the International Baccalaureate Diploma in Ontario: Diffusion, pilot study and prospective research. Caribbean Journal of Education, 35(4), 341-375. Retrieved from http://www.jstor.org/stable/canajeducrevucan.35.4.341

Tarique, I., & Weisbord, E. (2013). Antecedents of dynamic cross-cultural competence in adult third culture kids (ATKS). Journal of Global Mobility, 1(2), 139-160. doi:10/1108/JGM-12-2012-0021

Tate, S. A. (2014). Racial affective economies, disalienation and 'race made ordinary.' Ethnic and Racial Studies, 37(13), 2475-249. doi:10.1080/01419870.2 013.821146 Taylor, S. (2014). Globally-minded students: defining, measuring and developing intercultural sensitivity. International Schools Journal, 33(2), 26-34. Retrieved from http://academicguides.waldenu.edu/ library/ProQuest

Toffle, M. E. (2014). Cross-cultural website analysis as a method for teaching intercultural competence in the university English Program. In 5th World Conference on Educational Sciences, Procedia - Social and Behavioral Sciences, 116, 3524-3535. doi:10.1016/j.sbspro.2014.01.797

Tomlinson, C. A., & Jarvis, J. M. (2014). Case studies of success: Supporting academic success for students with high potential from ethnic minority and economically disadvantaged backgrounds. Journal for the Education of the Gifted, 37(3), 191- 219. doi:10.1177/0162353214540826

Tomlinson-Clarke, S. (2003). Multiculturalism and the Therapeutic Process. Psychotherapy Research, 13(3), 397–399. https://doi.org/10.1093/ptr/kpg034

Torfing, J. (1999). New theories of discourse : Laclau, Mouffe, and Zoizoek. Blackwell Publishers.

Trask-Tate, A., Cunningham, M., & Francois, S. (2014). The role of racial socialization in promoting the academic expectations of African American adolescents: Realities in a Posi-Brown Era. The Journal of Negro Education, 83(3), 281-299, 425, 427. doi:10.7709/jnegroeducation.83.3.0281

Trungpa, Chögyam & Giimian, Carolyn Rose. (2019). Shambhala : the sacred path of the warrior. Shambhala Publications, Inc.

Truong, M., Paradies, Y., & Priest, N. (2014). Interventions to improve cultural competence in healthcare: A systematic review of reviews. BMC Health Services Research, 14(1), 1-31. doi:10.1186/1472-6963-14-99

Tubbs, N. (2008). Education in Hegel. Continuum.

Turnsek, D. (2013). Enjoying cultural differences assists teachers in learning about diversity and equality: An evaluation of antidiscrimination and diversity training. CEPS Journal: Center for Educational Policy Studies Journal, 3(4), 117-138. Retrieved from http://academicguides.waldenu.edu/library/ProQuest

United Nations Development Programme (UNDP) (2002). Assessing connection between micro and macro level issues meeting. Retrieved from: http://web.undp.org/evaluation/documents/micro-macro.pdf

Uzpaliene, D., & Vaiciuniene, V. (2012). European dimension and multilingual functioning in higher education: Erasmus students' experience. Study about Languages, 20, 1777. doi:10.5755/j01.sal.0.20.1777

Van der Wurff, R., & Schoebach, K. (2014). Civic and citizen demands of news media and journalists: What does the audience expect from good journalism? Journalism and Mass Communication Quarterly, 91(3), 433-451. doi:10.1177/1077699014538974

Visser, A. (2015). State-funded activism: Lessons from civil society organizations in Ireland. Studies in Social Justice, 9(2), 231-243. Retrieved from http://academicguides.waldenu.edu/library/EBSCO

Vogel, J. (2015). Understanding language awareness in the first language teaching in Slovenia as a "traditional monocultural" society. Journal of Language and Cultural Education, 3(2), 22-31. doi:10.1515/jolace-2015-0011.

Von Bergen, C. W., Bressler, M. S., & Collier, G. (2012). Creating a culture and climate of civility in a sea of intolerance. Journal of Organizational Culture, Communications & Conflict, 16(2), 95-114. Retrieved from http://academicguides.waldenu.edu/library/

ProQuest

Von Bergen, C. W., Von Bergen, B. A., Stubblefield, C., & Bandow, D. (2012). Authentic tolerance: between forbearance and acceptance. Journal of Cultural Diversity, 19(4), 111-117. Retrieved from http://academicguides. waldenu.edu/library/ProQuest

Wang, C., & Wu, X. (2014). Volunteers' motivation, satisfaction, and management in large-scale events: An empirical test from the 2010 Shanghai World Expo. Voluntas, 25(3), 754-771. doi:10.1007/s11266-013-9350-0

Watson, J. R., Siska, P., & Wolfe, R. L. (2013). Assessing gains in language proficiency, cross-cultural competence, and regional awareness during study abroad: A preliminary study. Foreign Language Annals, 46(1), 62-79. doi:10.1111/flan.1201

Watt, K., Abbott, P., & Reath, J. (2015). Cultural competency training of GP registrars – exploring the views of GP supervisors. International Journal for Equity in Health, 14, 1-10. doi:10.1186/s12939-015-0226-3

Weissenstein, A., Ligges, S., Brouwer, B., Marschall, B., & Friederichs, H. (2014). Measuring the ambiguity tolerance of medical students: A cross-sectional study from the first to sixth academic years. BMC Family Practice, 15, 6. doi:10.1186/1471-2296-15-6

Wheeler, Harvey, ed. *Beyond The Punitive Society*.

Operant Conditioning: Social and Political Aspects. Wildwood House, 1973

Wilby, K. J., Taylor, J., Khalifa, S. I., & Jorgenson, D. (2015). A course-based cross-cultural interaction among pharmacy students in Qatar and Canada. American Journal of Pharmaceutical Education, 79(2), 26. doi:0.5688/ajpe79226

Williams, R. (1983). Culture and society, 1780-1950. Columbia University Press.

Williamson, J. M., Rink, J. A., & Hewin, D. H. (2012). The portrayal of bariatric surgery in the UK print media. Obesity Surgery, 22(11), 1690-1694. doi:10.1007/s11695-012-0701-5

Wilson, H. F. (2014). The possibilities of tolerance: Intercultural dialogue in a multicultural Europe. Environment and Planning D: Society and Space, 32(5), 852-868. doi:10.1068/d13063p

Wolcott, H. F. (1994). Transforming qualitative data: Description, analysis, and interpretation. Thousand Oaks, CA: Sage.

Wolf, C. A. (2012/2013). Going deep: Service-learning and human rights education. Journal for the Study of Peace and Conflict, 37-41. Retrieved from http://academicguides.waldenu.edu/library/EBSCO

Wood, M. J., & Atkins, M. (2006). Immersion in another culture: One strategy for increasing cultural competence. Retrieved from http://academicguides. waldenu.edu/library/ProQuest

Wright, E., & Lee, M. (2014). Developing skills for youth in the 21st century: The role of elite International Baccalaureate Diploma Programme schools in China. International Review of Education, 60, 199-216. doi:10.1007/s11159-014-9404-6

Xue, J. (2014). Cultivating intercultural communication competence through culture teaching. Theory and Practice in Language Studies, 4(7), 1492-1498. doi:10.4304/tpls.4.7.1492-1498

Ye, H. (2013). Developing teachers' cultural competence: application of appreciative inquiry in ESL teacher education. Teacher development, 17(1), 55-71. do i:10.1080/13664530.2012.753944

Yulong, Li. (2013). Cultivating student global competence: A pilot experimental study. Decision Sciences Journal of Innovative Education, 11(1), 125-143. doi:10.1111/j.1540-4609.2012.00371.x

Zarate, M. A., Shaw, M., Marquez, J. A., & Biagas, D. (2012). Cultural inertia: The effects of cultural change on intergroup relations and the self-concept. Journal of Experimental Social Psychology, 48(3), 634-645. doi:10.1016/j.jesp.2011.12.014

Zhang, J. (2014). Review of the Intercultural Development Inventory Manual (Vol. 3). Journal of Psychoeducational Assessment, 32(2), 178-183. Retrieved from http://academicguides.waldenu.edu/library/EBSCO

Zhao, H., Coombs, S., & Hong, C. (2014). A tale of change: China's cultural initiatives for security and identity. Seton Hall Journal of Diplomacy and International Relations, 15(2), 51-63. Retrieved from http://academicguides.waldenu.edu/library/GoogleScholar

Žižek, S. (2013). Less than nothing : Hegel and the shadow of dialectical materialism. Verso Books.

Zizek, S. & Hanlon, C.. (2001). Psychoanalysis and the Post-Political: An Interview with Slavoj Zizek. New Literary History, 32(1), 1–21. https://doi.org/10.1353/nlh.2001.0004

About The Author

Garfield Vernon, Ph.D., is an administrator,
author, educator, researcher, trainer, world
traveler and the recipient of many professional
and academic awards. He has served at the
United Nations, and been Vice President of an
international non-profit organization. A celebrated
speaker and university lecturer, Dr. Vernon
has presented before many world leaders.
He resides in Washington, D.C.

CONTACT

Readers wishing to send their comments
to Dr. Garfield Vernon, and/or institutions
or members of the press wishing to
engage Dr. Vernon for interviews,
presentations or speaking engagements
should contact the author at:

drgarfieldvernon@garfieldvernon.com

Pascal Editions 2022

Made in the USA
Middletown, DE
18 November 2023

42881727R00194